WALKING THROUGH
BRITTANY

Titles in the Footpaths of Europe Series

Normandy and the Seine
Walking through Brittany
Walks in Provence
Coastal Walks: Normandy and Brittany
Walking the Pyrenees
Walks in the Auvergne

WALKING THROUGH
BRITTANY

Translated by Jane Chalk, Helen McPhail
and Robyn Marsack
Translation co-ordinator: Ros Schwartz

Robertson McCarta

The publishers thank the following people for their help with this book: Isabelle Daguin, Philippe Lambert, Vicky Hayward, Gianna Rossi, Tessa Hatts,Eileen Cadman, Linda Osband.

First published in 1989 by

Robertson McCarta Limited
122 King's Cross.
London WC1X 9DS

in association with

Fédération Française de la Randonnée Pédestre
8 Avenue Marceau
75008 Paris

© Robertson McCarta Limited
© Fédération Française de Randonnée Pédestre
© Maps, Institut Geographique National (French Official Survey)
  and Robertson McCarta Limited.

Managing Editor Jackie Jones
Series design by Prue Bucknell
Production by Grahame Griffiths
Typeset by The Robertson Group, Llandudno
Planning Map by Robertson Merlin

Printed and bound in Hong Kong

British Library Cataloguing in Publication Data

Walking through Brittany. — (Footpaths of Europe).
   1. France. Brittany. Visitors' guides
   I. Series

   914.4'104838

   ISBN 1 — 85365-160-5

CONTENTS

A note from the publisher

The books in this French Walking Guide series are produced in association and with the help of the Fédération Française de la Randonnée Pédestre (French ramblers' association) — generally known as the FFRP.

The FFRP is a federal organisation and is made up of regional, local and many other associations and bodies that form its constituent parts. Individual membership is through these various local organisations. The FFRP therefore acts as an umbrella organisation overseeing the waymarking of footpaths, training and the publishing of the Topoguides, detailed guides to the Grande Randonnée footpaths.

There are at present about 170 Topoguides in print, compiled and written by local members of the FFRP, who are responsible for waymarking the walks — so they are well researched and accurate.

We have translated the main itinerary descriptions, amalgamating and adapting several Topoguides to create new regional guides. We have retained the basic Topoguide structure, indicating length and times of walks, and the Institut Géographique National (official French survey) maps overlaid with the routes.

The information contained in this guide is the latest available at the time of going to print. However, as publishers we are aware that this kind of information is continually changing and we are anxious to enhance and improve the guides as much as possible. We encourage you to send us suggestions, criticisms and those little bits of information you may wish to share with your fellow walkers. Our address is: Robertson McCarta, 122 King's Cross Road, London WC1X 9DS.

We shall be happy to offer a free copy of any one of these books to any reader whose suggestions are subsequently incorporated into a new edition.

It is possible to create a variety of routes by referring to the walks above and to the planning map (inside the front cover). Transport and accommodation are listed in the alphabetical index in the back of the book.

KEY

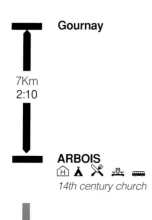

Gournay

This example shows that it is 7km from Gournay to Arbois to take 2 hours, 10 minutes.

7Km
2:10

ARBOIS

14th century church

Arbois has a variety of facilities, including hotels and buses. Hotel addresses and bus/train connections may be listed in the index at the back of the book.

a grey arrow indicates an alternative route that leaves and returns to the main route.

Detour

indicates a short detour off the route to a town with facilities or to an interesting sight.

Symbols:

hotel;
youth hostel, hut or refuge;
camping;
restaurant;
cafe;

shops;
railway station;
buses;
ferry;
tourist information

THE FOOTPATHS OF FRANCE

by Robin Neillands

Why should you go walking in France? Well, walking is fun and as for France, Danton summed up the attractions of that country with one telling phrase: 'Every man has two countries,' he said, 'his own . . . and France.' That is certainly true in my case and I therefore consider it both a pleasure and an honour to write this general introduction to these footpath guides to France. A pleasure because walking in or through France is my favourite pastime, an honour because these excellent English language guides follow in the course set by those Topo-guides published in French by the Fédération Française pour la Randonnée Pédestre, which set a benchmark for quality that all footpath guides might follow. Besides, I believe that good things should be shared and walking in France is one of the most pleasant activities I know.

I have been walking in France for over thirty years. I began by rambling — or rather ambling — through the foothills of the Pyrenees, crossing over into Spain past the old Hospice de France, coming back over the Somport Pass in a howling blizzard, which may account for the fact that I totally missed two sets of frontier guards on both occasions. Since then I have walked in many parts of France and even from one end of it to the other, from the Channel to the Camargue, and I hope to go on walking there for many years to come.

The attractions of France are legion, but there is no finer way to see and enjoy them than on foot. France has two coasts, at least three mountain ranges — the Alps, Pyrenees and the Massif Central — an agreeable climate, a great sense of space, good food, fine wines and, believe it or not, a friendly and hospitable people. If you don't believe me, go there on foot and see for yourself. Walking in France will appeal to every kind of walker, from the day rambler to the backpacker, because above all, and in the nicest possible way, the walking in France is well organised, but those Francophiles who already know France well will find it even more pleasurable if they explore their favourite country on foot.

The GR system

The Grande Randonnée (GR) footpath network now consists of more than 40,000 kilometres (25,000 miles) of long-distance footpath, stretching into every part of France, forming a great central sweep around Paris, probing deeply into the Alps, the Pyrenees, and the volcanic cones of the Massif Central. This network, the finest system of footpaths in Europe, is the creation of that marvellously named organisation, *la Fédération Française de Randonnée Pédestre, Comité National des Sentiers de Grande Randonnée,* which I shall abbreviate to FFRP-CNSGR. Founded in 1948, and declaring that, *'un jour de marche, huit jours de santé,* the FFRP-CNSGR has flourished for four decades and put up the now familiar red-and -white waymarks in every corner of the country. Some of these footpaths are classic walks, like the famous GR65, *Le Chemin de St. Jacques,* the ancient Pilgrim Road to Compostela, the TMB, the *Tour du Mont Blanc,* which circles the mountain through France, Switzerland and Italy, or the 600-mile long GR3, the *Sentier de la Loire,* which runs from the Ardèche to the Atlantic, to give three examples from the hundred or so GR trails available. In addition there is an abundance of GR du Pays or regional footpaths, like the *Sentier de la Haute Auvergne,* and the *Sentier Tour des Monts d'Aubrac.* A 'Tour' incidentally, is usually a circular walk. Many of these regional or provincial GR trails are charted and waymarked in red-and-yellow by local outdoor organisations such as ABRI (Association Bretonne des Relais et Itineraires) for Brittany, or CHAMINA for the Massif Central. The walker in France will soon become familiar with all these footpath networks, national, regional or local, and find them the perfect way into the heart and heartland of France. As a little bonus, the GR networks are expanding all the time, with the detours — or *varientes* — off the main route eventually linking with other GR paths or *varientes* and becoming GR trails in their own right.

Walkers will find the GR trails generally well marked and easy to follow, and they have two advantages over the footpaths commonly encountered in the UK. First, since they are laid out by local people, they are based on intricate local knowledge of the local sights. If there is a fine view, a mighty castle or a pretty village on your footpath route, your footpath through France will surely lead you to it. Secondly, all French footpaths are usually well provided with a wide range of comfortable country accommodation, and you will discover that the local people, even the farmers, are well used to walkers and greet them with a smile, a *'Bonjour'* and a *'bonne route'*.

Terrain and Climate

As a glance at these guides or any Topoguide will indicate. France has a great variety of terrain. France is twice the size of the UK and many natural features are also on a larger scale. There are three main ranges of mountains, the Alps contain the highest mountain in Europe, the Pyrenees go up to 10,000 ft, the Massif Central peaks to over 6000 ft, and there are many similar ranges with hills which overtop our highest British peak, Ben Nevis. On the other hand, the Auvergne and the Jura have marvellous open ridge walking, the Cévennes are steep and rugged, the Ardeche and parts of Provence are hot and wild, the Île de France, Normandy, Brittany and much of Western France is green and pleasant, not given to extremes. There is walking in France for every kind of walker, but given such a choice the wise walker will consider the complications of terrain and weather before setting out, and go suitably equipped.

France enjoys three types of climate: continental, oceanic, and mediterranean. South of the Loire it will certainly be hot to very hot from mid-April to late September. Snow can fall on the mountains above 4000 ft from mid-October and last until May, or even lie year-round on the tops and in couloirs; in the high hills an ice-axe is never a frill. I have used one by the Brêche de Roland in the Pyrenees in mid-June.

Wise walkers should study weather maps and forecasts carefully in the week before they leave for France, but can generally expect good weather from May to October, and a wide variety of weather — the severity depending on the terrain — from mid-October to late Spring.

Accommodation

The walker in France can choose from a wide variety of accommodation with the asurance that the walker will always be welcome. This can range from country hotels to wild mountain pitches, but to stay in comfort, many walkers will travel light and overnight in the comfortable hotels of the *Logis de France* network.

Logis de France: The *Logis de France* is a nationwide network of small, family-run country hotels, offering comfortable accommodation and excellent food. *Logis* hotels are graded and can vary from a simple, one-star establishment, with showers and linoleum, to a four- or five-star *logis* with with gastronomic menus and deep pile-carpets. All offer excellent value for money, and since there are over 5000 scattered across the French countryside, they provide a good focus for a walking day. An annual guide to the *Logis* is available from the French Government Tourist Office, 178 Piccadilly, London W1V 0AL, Tel (01) 491 7622.

Gîtes d'Etape: A *gîte d'étape* is best imagined as an unmanned youth hostel for outdoor folk of all ages. They lie along the footpath networks and are usually signposted or listed in the guides. They can be very comfortable, with bunk beds, showers, a well equipped kitchen, and in some cases they have a warden, a *guardien*, who may offer meals. *Gîtes de étape* are designed exclusively for walkers, climbers, cyclists, cross country skiers or horse-riders. A typical price (1989) would be Fr.25 for one night. *Gîtes de étape* should not be confused with a *Gîte de France*. A *gîte* — usually signposted as *'Gite de France'* — is a country cottage available for a holiday let, though here too, the owner may be more than willing to rent it out as overnight accommodation.

Youth hostels: Curiously enough, there are very few youth hostels in France outside the main towns. A full list of the 200 or so available can be obtained from the Youth Hostel Association (YHA), Trevelyan House, St. Albans, Herts AL1 2DY.

Pensions or cafes: In the absence of an hotel, a *gîte d'étape* or a youth hostel, all is not lost. France has plenty of accommodation and an enquiry at the village cafe or bar will usually produce a room. The cafe/hotel may have rooms or suggest a nearby pension or a *chambre d'hôte*. Prices start at around Fr.50 for a room, rising to say, Fr.120. (1989 estimate).

Chambres d'hôte: A *chambre d'hôte* is a guest room, or, in English terms, a bed-and-breakfast, usually in a private house. Prices range from about Fr.60 a night. *Chambres d'hôte* signs are now proliferating in the small villages of France and especially if you can speak a little French are an excellent way to meet the local people. Prices (1989) are from, say, Fr.70 for a room, not per person.

Abris: Abris, shelters or mountain huts can be found in the mountain regions, where they are often run by the *Club Alpin Francais,* an association for climbers. They range from the comfortable to the primitive, are often crowded and are sometimes reserved for members. Details from the Club Alpin Francais, 7 Rue la Boétie, Paris 75008, France.

Camping: French camp sites are graded from one to five star, but are generally very good at every level, although the facilities naturally vary from one cold tap to shops, bars and heated pools. Walkers should not be deterred by the *'Complet'* (Full) sign on the gate or office window: a walker's small tent will usually fit in somewhere. *Camping à la ferme,* or farm camping, is increasingly popular, more primitive — or less regimented — than the official sites, but widely available and perfectly adequate. Wild camping is officially not permitted in National Parks, but unofficially if you are over 1500m away from a road, one hour's walk from a *gîte* or campsite, and where possible ask permission, you should have no trouble. French country people will always assist the walker to find a pitch.

The law for walkers
The country people of France seem a good deal less concerned about their 'rights' than the average English farmer or landowner. I have never been ordered off land in France or greeted with anything other than friendliness . . . maybe I've been lucky. As a rule, walkers in France are free to roam over all open paths and tracks. No

decent walker will leave gates open, trample crops or break down walls, and taking fruit from gardens or orchards is simply stealing. In some parts of France there are local laws about taking chestnuts, mushrooms (and snails), because these are cash crops. Signs like *Réserve de Chasse*, or *Chasse Privé* indicate that the shooting is reserved for the landowner. As a general rule, behave sensibly and you will be tolerated everywhere, even on private land.

The country code
Walkers in France should obey the *Code du Randonneur.*

- Love and respect nature.
- Avoid unnecessary noise.
- Destroy nothing.
- Do not leave litter.
- Do not pick flowers or plants.
- Do not disturb wildlife.
- Re-close all gates.
- Protect and preserve the habitat.
- No smoking or fires in the forests. (This rule is essential and is actively enforced by foresters and police).
- Respect and understand the country way of life and the country people.
- Think of others as you think of yourself.

Transport
Transportation to and within France is generally excellent. There are no less than nine Channel ports: Dunkirk, Calais, Boulogne, Dieppe, Le Havre, Caen/Ouistreham, Cherbourg, Saint-Malo and Roscoff, and a surprising number of airports served by direct flights from the UK. Although some of the services are seasonal, it is often possible to fly direct to Toulouse, Poitiers, Nantes, Perpignan, Montpellier, indeed to many provincial cities, as well as Paris and such obvious destinations as Lyon and Nice. Within France the national railway, the SNCF, still retains a nationwide network. Information, tickets and a map can be obtained from the SNCF. France also has a good country bus service and the *gare routière* is often placed just beside the railway station. Be aware though, that many French bus services only operate within the *département,* and they do not generally operate from one provincial city to the next. I cannot encourage people to hitch-hike, which is both illegal and risky, but walkers might consider a taxi for their luggage. Almost every French village has a taxi driver who will happily transport your rucksacks to the next night-stop, fifteen to twenty miles away, for Fr.50 a head or even less.

Money
Walking in France is cheap, but banks are not common in the smaller villages, so carry a certain amount of French money and the rest in traveller's cheques or Eurocheques, which are accepted everywhere.

Clothing and equipment
The amount of clothing and equipment you will need depends on the terrain, the length of the walk, the time of your visit, the accommodation used. Outside the mountain areas it is not necessary to take the full range of camping or backpacking gear. I once walked across France from the Channel to the Camargue along the Grande Randonneé footpaths in March, April and early May and never needed to use any of the camping gear I carried in my rucksack because I found hotels

everywhere, even in quite small villages.

Essential items are:
In summer: light boots, a hat, shorts, suncream, lip salve, mosquito repellent, sunglasses, a sweater, a windproof cagoule, a small first-aid kit, a walking stick.
In winter: a change of clothing, stormproof outer garments, gaiters, hat, lip salve, a companion.
In the mountains at any time: large-scale maps (1:25,000), a compass, an ice-axe. In winter, add a companion and ten-point crampons.
At any time: a phrase book, suitable maps, a dictionary, a sense of humour.

The best guide to what to take lies in the likely weather and the terrain. France tends to be informal, so there is no need to carry a jacket or something smart for the evenings. I swear by Rohan clothing, which is light, smart and fuctional. The three things I would never go without are light, well-broken-in boots and several pairs of loop-stitched socks, and my walking stick.

Health hazards:
Health hazards are few. France can be hot in summer, so take a full water-bottle and refill at every opportunity. A small first-aid kit is sensible, with plasters and 'mole-skin' for blisters, but since prevention is better than the cure, loop-stitched socks and flexible boots are better. Any French chemist — a *pharmacie* — is obliged to render first-aid treatment for a small fee. These pharmacies can be found in most villages and large towns and are marked by a green cross.

Dogs are both a nuisance and a hazard. All walkers in France should carry a walking stick to fend off aggressive curs. Rabies — *la rage* — is endemic and any-one bitten must seek immediate medical advice. France also possesses two types of viper, which are common in the hill areas of the south. In fairness, although I found my walking stick indispensable, I must add that in thirty years I have never even seen a snake or a rabid dog. In case of real difficulty, dial 17 for the police and the ambulance.

Food and wine
One of the great advantages with walking in France is that you can end the day with a good meal and not gain an ounce. French country cooking is generally excellent and good value for money, with the price of a four-course menu starting at about Fr.45. The ingredients for the mid-day picnic can be purchased from the village shops and these also sell wine. Camping-Gaz cylinders and cartridges are widely available, as is 2-star petrol for stoves. Avoid naked fires.

Preparation
The secret of a good walk lies in making adequate preparations before you set out. It pays to be fit enough to do the daily distance at the start. Much of the necessary information is contained in this guide, but if you need more, look in guidebooks or outdoor magazines, or ask friends.

The French
I cannot close this introduction without saying a few words about the French, not least because the walker in France is going to meet rather more French people than, say, a motorist will, and may even meet French people who have never met a foreigner before. It does help if the visitor speaks a little French, even if only to say *'bonjour'* and *'Merci'* and *'S'il vous plait'*. The French tend to be formal so it pays to

be polite, to say 'hello', to shake hands. I am well aware that relations between France and England have not always been cordial over the last six hundred years or so, but I have never met with hostility of any kind in thirty years of walking through France. Indeed, I have always found that if the visitor is prepared to meet the French halfway, they will come more than halfway to greet him or her in return, and are both friendly and hospitable to the passing stranger.

As a final tip, try smiling. Even in France, or especially in France, a smile and a *'pouvez vous m'aider?'* (Can you help me?) will work wonders. That's my last bit of advice, and all I need do now is wish you *'Bonne Route'* and good walking in France.

WALKING THROUGH BRITTANY

By Toby Oliver

Brittany is France's Cornwall - not only do they say that a Breton speaking Breton can understand a Cornishman speaking Cornish but the country and coastline are very similar. Brittany's 1,200 kilometres of coastline feature beautiful, unspoilt, sandy beaches, little fishing ports nestling in the Abers and inlets, wild rocky sections facing the Atlantic rollers and larger humming resorts. Inland it is mainly rolling green country littered with villages, hamlets and farms, wood, forests, rivers and moorland, depending on which part you are in. All excellent walking country!

What is more, Brittany is not that far away: daily, year-round ferry services operating from Portsmouth to Saint-Malo and Plymouth to Roscoff make getting there easy.

The province shares strong cultural and historic links with Britain and is definitely a place to go if you want to feel at home. The Bretons like the British. After all, when the 400 years of Roman rule which followed Julius Caesar's takeover in 56BC were over it was the Celts, driven out of Britain by raiding Saxons, who arrived in Armorica or 'the land facing the sea' and renamed their new homeland 'Little Britain', later shortened to Brittany.

Legends link Britain and Brittany and, of them all, King Arthur and his Knights must be one of the most vivid - romance, bravery, violence, sorcery and dastardly plotting. Apparently a lot of this went on in Brittany when the King and his followers arrived in search of the Holy Grail. Poor Merlin met his match in the Forest of Broceliande (now called the Forêt de Paimpont) where he was condemned to a living tomb of stone.

But enough of legends and the past. Modern Brittany has dragged itself out of the doldrums of the 50s and early 60s when its farming community was not thriving to say the least! Today it is one of the most affluent regions in the whole of France, with a healthy economy based on agriculture, fishing and tourism. Britain takes their farm produce and in return sends them a large percentage of their annual tourist intake.

The routes

This book contains a great variety of walking routes, different lengths through different areas of Brittany. All are designed to enable you to see the best of this beautiful region.

I have walked many of the paths described here: a four-day walk north from Rennes, the Brittany capital, ending up in Mont-Saint-Michel; another four-day stroll between Mont-Saint-Michel and Saint-Malo with a detour inland to Dol de Bretagne. Redon is the end of another attractive walk south from Rennes, down the pretty valley of the River Vilaine. From there you can pick up the GR347 Val d'Oust au pays de Gallo route along the Canal de Nantes to Josselin - probably one of the best known places in Brittany with its famous castle of the Rohan family.

This is a meeting point of many footpaths. You can go north-west via Pontivy to Carhaix, skirting the western end of the Forêt de Lanonée across the rolling hills and valleys of inland Morbihan and southern Côtes du Nord.

In the very centre of Brittany, Pontivy stands on the River Blavet and came to prominence when Napoleon built the canal between Brest and

Nantes to pass through the town which was just about the half way point. At the time the town was called Napoléonville, but after Waterloo the town reverted to its original name. North of the town lies the Lac de Guerlédan which is one of the finest sights of inland Brittany. At the eastern end of the lake is Mur de Bretagne, where the great oak trees inspired the French painter Corot in the mid-nineteenth century.

From here the footpath takes you north across the pleasant undulating green countryside of the Côtes du Nord, towards Lannion.

Another longer circular walk starts and finishes at Saint-Brieuc, the administrative centre of the Côtes du Nord, which occupies a privileged position as a promontory above two valleys. The walk goes south east to Dinan which is well worth exploring: stroll round its winding streets bordered with 15th, 16th and 17th century houses, its ramparts and towers.

Food

All this exercise is obviously going to promote the hunger pangs. There are some delicious Breton dishes and some famous ones. Who knows that *Lobster à l'Armoricaine* was named after the area of Brittany known as Armorique? Seafood is found in abundance with oysters, langoustine and all sorts of shellfish piled high on a *plat de fruits de mer* which can all be washed down by crisp dry Muscadet. Brittany is big in pigs, so pork is features strongly on most menus, with pork with prunes being a traditional dish which should satisfy most appetites. It is a rich and warming meal, to be washed down by some local Breton cider. The vegetables - potatoes, cauliflowers, carrots, artichokes are unbeatable for quality and freshness.

It always amazes me what terrific value for money eating out in France is. The little villages and towns you come across walking in Brittany will probably have

restaurants, little hotels or auberges, offering not only a bed for the night but a selection of menus, many of which will start at only 40 or 50 francs. Spot the places without too many GB plated cars outside but full of Bretons, and it is a safe bet you will get a good, value for money meal.

The weather tends to follow a similar pattern to the southern part of England - though I think it would be fair to say that Brittany has more sunshine than the UK and is a few degrees warmer.

As for transport, once you have crossed the channel, good bus or rail links will take you to most main centres and the start line for the walks described in this book (the French Railways Office in Piccadilly, London: 01-409 1224 is most helpful regarding train times, routes etc.).

So, armed with this book, an extra map perhaps, and maybe a phrase book in case the French is a bit rusty, walkers can put their best foot forward and make the most of this charming region just a short ferry ride away.

WALK 1

The GR39 route to Mont-Saint-Michel is both one of the shortest (100 kilometres) and one of the most varied GR paths. The first part, in two stages, goes through the rolling countryside of the Rennes basin. It crosses the state forests of Rennes and Haute-Sève, amidst beautiful beech plantations. The countryside is hollowed out as it approaches the valley of the Couesnon, with its steep, wooded banks which serve as the guideline for the footpath. This is country of granite, found in all types of construction, and also a country for hikers, with numerous circular walks. The descent towards the bay of Mont-Saint-Michel is common to all the routes. This last part is especially attractive and includes the forest of Ville-Cartier, as the silhouette of the Mont-Saint-Michel gradually dominates the landscape.

RENNES

Rennes has played an important role for many years as the regional capital. The former Parliament of Brittany, now the Palace of Justice, with its fine 17th century interior decoration; the old street saved from the fire of 1720; the avenues of the garden of Le Thabor.

4Km
1

The first stage of the GR39 route links Rennes to the gîte of La Lande Ragot, via the canal d'Ille-et-Rance as far as Betton, then across the forest of Rennes. If you start out from Rennes, this is a long section (28 kilometres); cutting through the forest only takes off 1 or 2 kilometres. Thus you can use hotels in Betton; save the first 12 kilometres along the towpath by leaving from Betton, which is well served by buses; or gain 2 extra kilometres by taking a coach from Rennes to Gahard, at the beginning of the forest of Rennes.

Leaving Rennes there is an interesting walk from the centre of town; you can reach the canal d'Ille-et-Rance by the little medieval streets of the old town. Walk along the Boulevard de Chézy, pass the youth hostel and continue north for a while on the towpath, where the markings are too unobtrusive to be useful.

Detour, *2 Km*
LES GAYEULLES

Shortly after a bridge under a road, at a junction, take the footpath from the `Tour de Rennes'.

The canal passes under various bridges, then runs alongside the town of Saint-Grégoire.

SAINT-GRÉGOIRE

8Km
2

Continue along the same bank, the looping path lined with trees. Pass beneath the Roulefort stud farm, go along by the Gasset lock, then the Centre de la Vallée, dominated by a chapel. It is a straight path to Betton.

BETTON
⌂ ✕ ⚖ 🚌 🚃

The ancient part of the town is found to the west of the canal, on the heights. The church has fine 16th century stained-glass.

2Km
0:30

LA PETITE HUBLAIS
🍷 🚃

5.5Km
1:30

This aqueduct, more than 200 years old, takes water from a tributary of the Couesnon, the Minette, to Rennes.

Crossroads of La Table
Detour, *15 mins,*
MI-FORÊT
🍷 🚃

Follow the road eastwards.

7Km
1:45

The GR leaves the canal on the right to go through La Levée, which is the last provisioning point for this stage of the walk. Cross the main road at a level crossing, and follow to the left a minor road near the railway lines. Leave this after about a kilometre, at a group of farms, for a gravel path to the left. You will come across the restored farm of La Hublais, then the houses and equestrian centre of La Petite Hublais.

The GR now goes through the state forest of Rennes (3,000 hectares) for some while. You go into the forest beneath fine beech trees, and the undergrowth is mainly holly. Where possible the footpath avoids the bridle paths. When you meet a small, straight ditch cross a bridle path, then walk down to the River Caleuvre. The path follows the winding course of this river upstream, crosses a lane, and then merges with a circular PR walk marked out in white circles (not shown on map). Go across recently planted areas, then cross two forest roads. Go north-east, and cross several streams to reach a large gap created by the aqueduct for the River Minette.

You then reach the crossroads of La Table.

Leaving the PR circular walk, follow the aqueduct path to the left. The GR, keeping close to the aqueduct, is joined by the PR Saint-Raoul circular walk. After a gentle climb, take the footpath on the left between plots 55 and 56; it is difficult to see this as it is behind a building. Cross a cycle path to reach the Étang des Maffrais, which is a popular leisure area. The GR skirts the left of the pond, takes the log footbridge then crosses a road opposite the entrance to the parking area. After an irregular path through the trees, you will find the aqueduct path again, which you follow for some time northwards. Leave it on the right to cross a main road, and continue opposite between plots 5 and 6, until you reach a forest road.

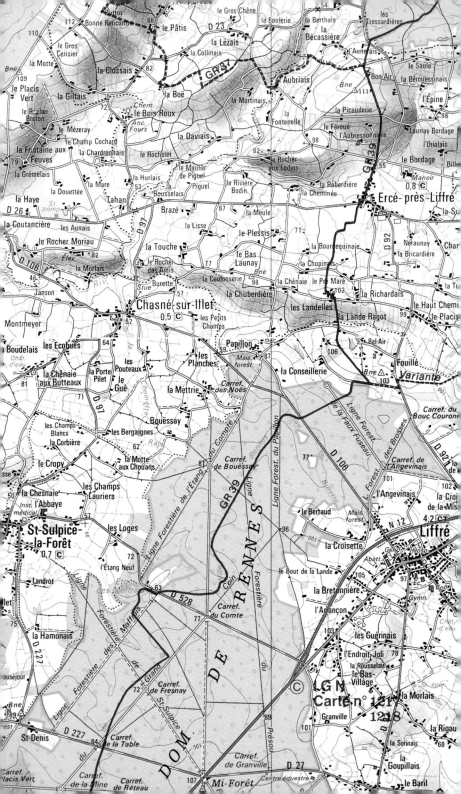

Forest Road
Detour, 45 mins,
LIFFRÉ
🏠 🅰 ✕ 🍷 🚌

0.5Km
0:10

*Follow the forest road
south-east; walk along to
the right of the campsite,
then turn left.*

North of the
Forest of Rennes

1Km
0:15

LA LANDE RAGOT
⌂

2Km
0:30

ERCÉ-PRÈS-LIFFRÉ
🍷 🚃 🚌

*The Château du Bordage
lies 500 metres to the right;
a few handsome buildings
and the 18th century ruins
remain.*

2Km
0:30

**La Croix-Saint-
Georges**
This is an old granite cross.

Continue north via two recently planted plots
to a minor road. You will meet the crossroads
200 metres on, to the right, where there is a
signpost. You are north of the forest of Rennes.

Alternative route to La Guibertière. To the
east, via the road, take the GR37, via the
forest of Liffré. The GR39 follows the dirt track
to the right, goes over a hill and meets La
Lande Ragot.

The path continues north to Landelles, where
the GR goes through the hamlet on the left,
then goes right just after the last house. This
path is in poor condition, and its repair is
planned. Eventually it may be bypassed, at
the expense of a detour of 1 kilometre via the
hamlet of Richardais, situated 400 metres
east of Les Landelles. The GR continues
downwards, sometimes on the public footpath
at the edge of a field to the village of Ercé-
près-Liffré.

Leave the village by the Gahard road, and
cross the Illet.

Shortly after the crossroads, cross the ditch
on the right and walk along an ancient Roman
way, very broad but overgrown, a passage
having been kept clear for hikers. It comes
out near a cross; continue opposite on a
gravel road to the Bel Air estate and the
crossroads of La Croix-Saint-Georges.

You will meet the GR37, whose west branch
continues towards the centre of Brittany.
Eastwards, the two GRs share a path for 4
kilometres to the crossroads of La Grande
Brèche.

The path goes down to Les Tressardières, at
the entrance to the state forest of Saint-
Aubin-du-Cormier (or the forest of Haute-
Sève). The route to La Grande Brèche goes
through a shooting range in the Lande d'Ouée.
On shooting days (excepting Wednesdays
and weekends), use of this route may be
forbidden, either by the military, or by notices.

In that case you must go by road to the northern edge of the forest, keeping close to it until you meet the GR again, a little before La Grande Brèche. At the entrance to the forest you will meet the Minette again, made into a canal, and covered over by a regular levee. Cross a former railway line, and you will join up with the yellow marking for the Gahard circular walk. To the left, the Blaireau rocks offer several beginners' climbs. The GR crosses the mound which continues on from these rocks affording a view to the north over the Gahard plain. It then goes on through beech trees. First of all walk along by the aqueduct, then do not miss the path which strikes out to the left.

4Km
1:0

Five standing stones are scattered to the right of the footpath, in the plots 48, 50 and 52.

The GR goes down a forest road, then returns to the northern edge of the forest.

Reverse route: on shooting days, keep to the edge of the forest until you come to the D92; follow this to the left to Les Tressardières.

Crossroads of La Grande Brèche

The GR37 continues straight on to the woods of Uzel, then to Saint-Aubin-du-Cormier and Vitré. The GR39 goes left towards Mézières.

Alternative route to Mézières. The route via the woods of Uzel is longer (14 kilometres rather than 6 kilometres), but much more picturesque. Go left in the woods at the end of the Vitré-Mézières route.

5Km
1:15

The GR39 crosses a road, then continues straight towards the north by the Charriére Fleurie avenue. Cross the Riclon, and leave first the forest and then the PR circular walk. A dirt track carries on, a little by road and then by the drive leading to the Château de la Sécardais. Go down to the left towards La Miennais.

Château de la Sécardais
Châteaubriand stayed here several times.

The GR continues north, passing the hamlet of Louinais. Turn right on to a narrow path, then shortly afterwards to the left along the edge of a field. Go through the turnstile into a wood, from which you suddenly emerge in the deep valley of the Couesnon.

Detour, *800m southeast,*
MÉZIÈRES-SUR-COUESNON
△ ✗ ⍱ ♨
The bell-tower is clearly visible from the plain.

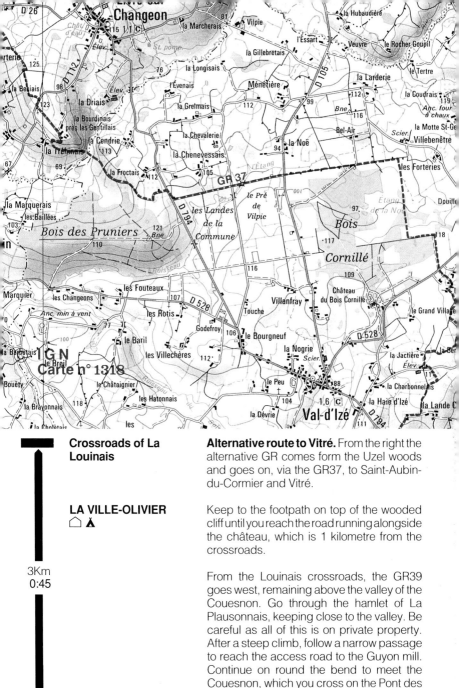

Crossroads of La Louinais

Alternative route to Vitré. From the right the alternative GR comes form the Uzel woods and goes on, via the GR37, to Saint-Aubin-du-Cormier and Vitré.

LA VILLE-OLIVIER
⌂ ⛺

Keep to the footpath on top of the wooded cliff until you reach the road running alongside the château, which is 1 kilometre from the crossroads.

3Km
0:45

From the Louinais crossroads, the GR39 goes west, remaining above the valley of the Couesnon. Go through the hamlet of La Plausonnais, keeping close to the valley. Be careful as all of this is on private property. After a steep climb, follow a narrow passage to reach the access road to the Guyon mill. Continue on round the bend to meet the Couesnon, which you cross on the Pont des Intrépides.

Pont des Intrépides

The site of Mézières-sur-Couesnon

At 30 kilometres from Rennes, Mézières offers a good number of opportunities for open-air activities: at the bottom of the valley there is the Couesnon, where canoe-kayaks go downstream to Antrain; on the north bank, there is rock-climbing for beginners, where climbers from the Breton section of the Club Alpin Français do their training; finally, in the south there is a great network of footpaths dotted over the wooded slope.

5Km
1:15

Detour, *15 mins,*
SAINT-CHRISTOPHE-DE-VALAINS

Three local circular walks, each less than an hour, keep within the site. The walk can extend to the whole day, going by the loop of Haute-Sève - 20 kilometres in length - by the alternative GR as far as the woods of Uzel, then via the forest of Haute-Sève as far as the Grande Brèche crossroads, before returning to the valley of the Couesnon. This loop runs beside another circuit of 18 kilometres via the neighbouring grove of Gahard.

Go left after the bridge on a footpath beside the water. Climb the Rofinière by a very narrow path. A series of dirt tracks look over the right bank of the Couesnon at first, then go off to the north-west. Cross the D20, then the hamlet of Les Landelles.

North of Les Landelles you will find a path, at present in very poor condition, called the `chemin des Anglais' (work under consideration). Make your way as best you can to a wayside cross, then the hamlet of La Basse Haie, where there is a `Chêne de la Liberté' (liberty oak). An increasingly picturesque path descends into the valley of

Charming village, with granite houses; outstanding church and wayside cross; weaving studio, with an exhibition.

The road to the right goes to Les Landelles. Return to the GR by the road from La Basse Haie, in order to avoid the bad road described above.

the Minette, near the mill of La Sourde.

Reverse route: go towards a house, and take the lightly marked footpath to the right after a small garden.

Cross a footbridge and climb through a wood. The GR is joined by blue and white markings for the `circuit du Tiercent'. Go through the Brimblin wood (private property; passage has kindly been authorised) and skirt a meadow by a fairly difficult path on the left. Come back towards the right, behind a hedge, towards the signpost marking the beginning of the alternative Romazy route.

Crossroads of Brimblin

With its network of surrounding footpaths, Chauvigné has become a Mecca for hikers in Brittany.

4Km
1

The GR39 goes right towards Chauvigné.

CHAUVIGNÉ
⌂

4Km
1:0

Château de Bonne-Fontaine

A handsome, 16th century building, with some fortifications. Notice in the courtyard a well with monolithic coping, and a stone basin. Permission has been granted for access to the park.

ANTRAIN-SUR-COUESNON
🏠 ⌂ 🛉 ✕ ⚓

12th century nave and transept of the church, which also has a fine Romanesque doorway.

LA FONTENELLE
🍷 ⚓

Circular walk, marked out

Alternative route via Romazy. This alternative route along the valley of the Couesnon offers a walk of more sustained interest, over a comparable distance, but it does not offer any shelter. Its beginning requires a little care. A succession of paths enables you to pass by La Jennerie, then via the fine houses of La Moisondaie. Go back up between the meadows.

The former mines of Brais are 1 kilometre to the right, with an original mining village, and a striking view of the confluence of the Minette and the Couesnon.

A marked alternative route joins the GR34 at the grotte d'Ardennes, the Ardennes cave. The two GRs are only 3.5 kilometres apart at this point.

The GR39 goes left (north) to Les Fossés by a path which is difficult at first, then becomes very pleasant along the boundary of the Château de Bonne-Fontaine.

To the north you will meet up with the suburbs of Antrain-sur-Couesnon. The GR goes along by the campsite, then the fairground. Go back up to the right, then soon left to find the junction with the GR34, near a wayside cross.

The rest of the GR, as far as Mont-Saint-Michel, is shared by all four itineraries.

To the west of the church there is a wayside cross, in the middle of a little road leading down towards the Couesnon. You cross the river by two old bridges. Turn right at the mill; leave the road shortly afterwards for a little footpath - scarcely visible - to the left (leaving the white markings behind). This footpath overlooks a deeply sunken path, the exit from which is unfortunately blocked. Continue up the footpath to the first houses of La Fontenelle. Turn left at the church.

Leave the village from the west by a good dirt road, which soon becomes surfaced. Cross the D155, and take a bad road opposite, then

in white dots.

leave it to cross a field. Pass through the hamlet of Ville-Neuve. Follow a minor road southwards, and turn right just after a rise, on to a dirt track as far as the edge of the forest.

The forest of Ville-Cartier

A beautiful state forest of 1,000 hectares.

The GR, sometimes accompanied by orange markings for a bridle path, proceeds westwards for some while, across several plantations of broad-leaved trees. From the crossroads of La Boutelais follow a sandy walk sometimes through the trees - to the crossroads of Haute-Coupelle. The GR continues through the forest amidst magnificent groves. You will come across the white dots marking a circular forest walk. Following this walk, you will pass by a handsome stone cross, the Croix de Montauge. The footpath goes down towards a lake; cross the stream which runs into it and walk along the east bank. At the crossing of another stream, head away from the lake towards the north-east.

13.5Km
3:30

Detour
THE FOREST MILL
✗ ♈

Continue round the lake by the forest path.

Cross the D155 again, then emerge from the forest near the farm of La Courbe. Going north, follow first a dirt track, then an avenue of conifers leading to the Maucrais farm. Go into the meadow to the right of the farm (private pathway; be sure to fasten the gate); walk along by the hedge on the left. Take the path as soon as possible; if it is too wet underfoot, walk alongside it, being careful of the crops. The path comes to the edge of the cliff which overlooks the Mont-Saint-Michel plain.

Before you step on this sunken path, from the path on the left take a look at the plain that you will be crossing, out of which the Mount emerges. The sunken path, often very deep, is muddy at the lowest part because of a spring. After walking for more than 100 metres at an altitude of less than 30 metres, you will reach the village of Vieux Viel.

VIEUX VIEL
♈ ⛉

Leave the village on a good road going north, followed by a short track. Turn right on to a little road which was formerly surfaced. You will meet a wider road, which you take to the left. (If it is raining heavily, you should continue along this road and rejoin the GR by turning right after the Bas Home.) Leave the road on

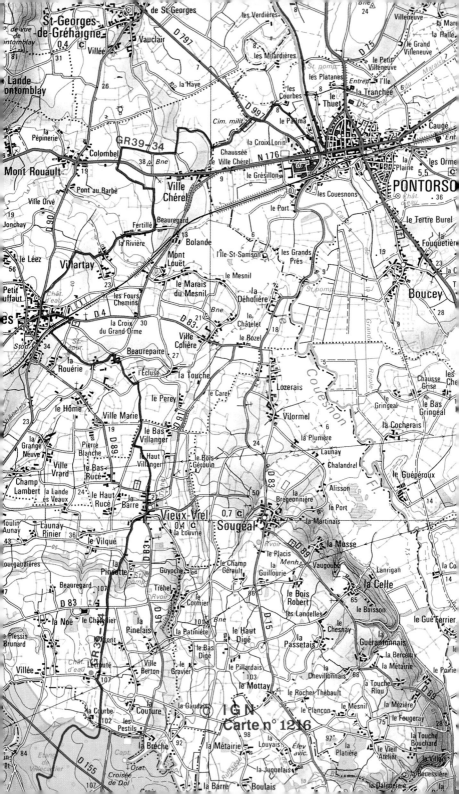

3.5Km
1:0

PLEINE-FOUGÈRES

4Km
1:0

PONTORSON

An important Channel town, the `door to the Mont-Saint-Michel'.

LA GOURMETTE

2Km
0:30

PONT DE BEAUVOIR

the right and go down towards a marsh, which you cross by a little bridge. Across a meadow you come to a narrow passage between the houses of Beaupaire. (See above for what to do if this way is flooded.) The GR proceeds towards the small town of Pleine-Fougères. Go right, between the railway line and the road, along a lane of *prunus* (pretty rose flowers in spring). Cross the level crossing.

Leave the town by the D90 in the north. Take a dirt track to the right. When it meets a minor road, go right and through the hamlets of Villartray and La Rivière. The path continues along the road - for about 2 kilometres in all - northwards. A little before the Pontorson-Saint-Malo road, you make a large detour west along dirt tracks. Cross the D176, then follow a path to the right. After a short tarmac stretch, you start on a series of paths winding across the plain. At the old Pontorson cemetery, you meet the main road, the D997. Follow this to the right, then turn left. Just before you reach the buildings, go right, along the edge of a field. A broader path meets the Couesnon in the suburbs of Pontorson.

The GR crosses the Couesnon, then immediately goes left. It runs alongside a campsite, then the right bank of a stream which has now been harnessed. Go north along the towpath for some time. The path departs from the river bank to skirt the municipal gîtes.

For those going directly to Mont-Saint-Michel, the path along the bank of the Couesnon is the most pleasant, although it goes through the racecourse complex. Walkers can decide when they reach it if this seems the best way to them.

After the riding school, follow the main road north for a bit, then return as soon as possible to the bank of the Couesnon, along by the racecourse. You will reach the Beauvoir bridge.

Continue north along the grassy bank of the Couesnon, to La Caserne, which marks the land's northern limit. Here the GR39 meets the GR22 coming from the east, and the GR34 which continues west, crossing a lock.

LA CASERNE
⌂ ⚠ ✕

4Km
1:0

MONT-SAINT-MICHEL
⌂ ⚓ 🚃 ⓘ

*For the walker with an hour
or two to spare, a visit to
the Mount, the `Marvel of
the West', is warmly
recommended.*

There are now only 2 kilometres to the Mount, which is linked to the land by a dyke. You can follow a little road below this dyke on the west side, or wander freely off the beaten track on the vast grassy stretches to the east.

After the entrance posterns, the Grande Rue (the only street) creates a striking medieval impression. You may turn off, at the church, to make a quieter tour. Returning westwards, terraced gardens overlook the entrance. From the circular path further uphill, there is a sweeping view south towards Pontorson. You can go on westwards to the Gabriel tower, from which you can see, beyond the Couesnon, the enormous grassy stretches you will later walk over. Returning eastwards, you will arrive at the entrance to the abbey. A grand staircase leads to the room from which the guided tours begin (lasting three-quarters of an hour).Go down again to reach the northern ramparts, from which you will discover a new aspect of the bay, looking towards the îlot de Tombelaine and the coast of Cotentin. Follow the ramparts to the towers at the entrance. It is interesting to devote half an hour to the tour of the Mount around the outside (if the tide permits), without straying too far from it.

Warning: Walking across the bay can be very dangerous: the tide comes in very suddenly and irregularly, and can quickly cut off your retreat; in other areas (quite far from the Mount) patches of sand, not visible to the uninitiated, cover up water holes and give way under your feet. These are the famous `sables mouvants' (shifting sands), which are by no means just legends!

WALK 2

The GR34c walk was originally part of the GR34, in the days when this was not marked between Dinard and Saint-Brieuc. It could also be included in a GR country walk or a route round the Rance estuary. The Rance is public maritime property up to the Châtelier lock, 5 kilometres north of Dinan: pedestrian right of way therefore applies, as it does round the coastline. So far, the path has been completed as far as the Pleurtuilt area.

There are, however, many good paths from Dinard to Minihic-sur-Rance. Beyond that point, the route sometimes follows dirt tracks which run near the sea, and sometimes actually runs along the shore itself. In the latter case, the going sometimes becomes very difficult, if not impossible, when the sea is right in. When this happens, you will just have to make your way through the fields or along the roads behind the coast, which are unmarked and may well be less interesting.

Signposting is a bit haphazard along the shore, as there are few posts for signs between the hard mud and the thorn bushes. Matters are also complicated by the fact that the tides around the Rance dam occur at different times from those in surrounding areas outside the influence of the dam. They are fixed by EDF (Electricité de France) according to demand for power, and can only be found out by looking in the local paper or asking EDF direct.

You need make very few preparations in advance to make a trip round the beautiful Rance countryside - a real inland sea - particularly for the central portion between Minihic and Plouër-sur-Rance. You may like to note that the return journey from Dinan to Saint-Malo can be made by boat.

LE MONT-SAINT-MICHEL BAY

This vast bay is an enchanted area, full of legends of vanished villages, and stories of the eternal struggle between the Archangel Michael and the Devil.

2Km
0:30

The area directly surrounding Le Mont-Saint-Michel is worth exploring, but only if the tide is right — it comes in very quickly and unevenly and can cut you off. There are also patches of sand which conceal deep troughs of water, indiscernible to the unpractised eye (the infamous 'shifting sands'),

The walk starts from the bay. Le Mont-Saint-Michel, called the 'Marvel of the West', is reached after a climb up granite cliffs. Go through the postern gates and walk down La Grande Rue. You can turn off the street when you get to the church to follow a quieter route. Arriving at the west gate, you can look down onto the entrance to the mount from terraced gardens. You also have a good view of the coast as it stretches inland (south) towards Pontorson. From Gabriel tower you can see westwards beyond the River Couesnon to the great grassy stretches of the polders. At the abbey entrance a magnificent staircase leads to the starting point for the guided tour (45 minutes). From the northern ramparts you can see the little island of Tombelaine and the Cotentin coastline.

As it leaves the mount, the GR follows the seawall south. This wall, built in 1897, has provoked a lot of controversy. It has caused sand to build up around the mount by preventing the sea from flowing freely round

which would leave you floundering.

LA CASERNE
🏠 ⌂ ⋀ ✗ 🚌

2Km
0:30

Pont de Beauvoir
Detour *30 mins*
LE MOIDREY
⌂

9Km
2:15

Junction of two dykes

8Km
2:0

the island, and it may eventually be replaced by a bridge. If you want to avoid walking along a stretch of road, take a bus from Mount-Saint-Michel railway station to La Caserne or Beauvoir bridge.

Beware! You must not cross the River Couesnon near La Caserne over the barrier floodgate. Any walkers who do so do it at their own risk. You have to make a detour via Beauvoir bridge.

Detour *(see left)*
Continue on the east bank of the Couesnon until just after the racecourse.

Cross the bridge, and turn right (north) following the GR34 along the west bank of the Couesnon back to the barrier floodgate opposite La Caserne (Remember: you are forbidden to cross this floodgate .) Beyond the floodgate there are no markings on the dyke. Follow the dyke westwards to the first crossroads, and turn right (north). The fertile polders behind the dyke were regained from the sea in the nineteenth century. The sea only comes up to the dyke at very high tides. There is a large stretch of grass outside the dyke, where salt-meadow sheep graze. The flat landscape is only broken by raised shepherd huts (do not go into them) and hunters' hides. It is worth exploring around the dyke, but also worth returning to the dyke every now and again to get a good view of Mont-Saint-Michel. There is a road on the left leading to Poulder Foulon farm 6 kilometres after the floodgate. Ignore this, and continue along the dyke for 1 kilometre, where you will find the remains of a landing stage, and another dyke running inland. The markings for the GR start again here.

Alternative route to Hirel and Dol.
This junction is the departure point for an unmarked alternative route leading to Hirel, and makes a circular route of 45 kilometres by joining up with the GR34 again at Hirel, and passing later through Dol-de-Bretagne. This walk to Hirel runs along the coastline, sometimes following the dyke, sometimes the roads. It is shown as a dotted line on the maps.

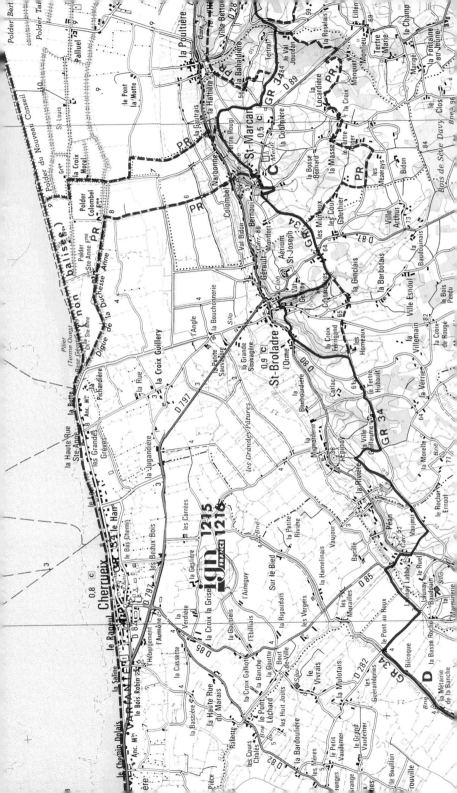

CHERRUEIX

See map on page 22

5Km
1:15

Detour, *15 mins*
L'AUMONE

LE VIVIER -SUR-MER

See map on page 24

2Km
0:30

HIREL

This is where you rejoin the GR34.

3Km
0:45

At the junction of the two dykes, the GR34 leaves the sea and turns left (south) along private dykes between the polders. Lined with poplar trees, these dykes are sometimes overgrown with tall grass, or scattered with grazing cattle and sheep. Make sure that you close all gates and stick to the set path. You then take the road leading away from the polders towards the hamlet of Quatre-Salines.

LE QUATRE-SALINES

The GR cuts across the road (D797) at a cluster of houses named Le Bas du Palais.

LE BAS DU PALAIS

You now find yourself at the foot of a cliff; the sea used to come in as far as this point before the polders were built. Take the road leading to Roz-sur-Couesnon, and turn off at the first hairpin bend along a rather overgrown path which wends its way through the scrub up to the public gardens at Roz-sur-Couesnon. From here, you have a magnificent view out over the polders and the long straight line of poplar trees to Mont-Saint-Michel in the distance, The GR now enters the market town of Roz-sur-Couesnon.

1Km
0:15

ROZ-SUR-COUESNON

Paul Feval based his work 'La Fée des Gréves (Fairy of the Shore) here. Bakers sell a curious flat loaf of bread, which they call 'tourteau' (cattle cake).

The GR heads west out of Roz-sur-Couesnon along the road, and then drops away to the left down an overgrown track and crosses a stream. Take the sunken path back up to the road, turn left and then follow a tarmac road of to the right (west) which climbs upwards to give you a good view of the bay. Further on it cuts across two roads and runs past a campsite. You come out close to the gîte at Saint-Marcan.

4Km
1:0

SAINT-MARCAN

The GR heads west out of Saint-Marcan. If you turn right and then left at the first crossroads, you can visit the 'Petit Mont-Saint-Michel', a

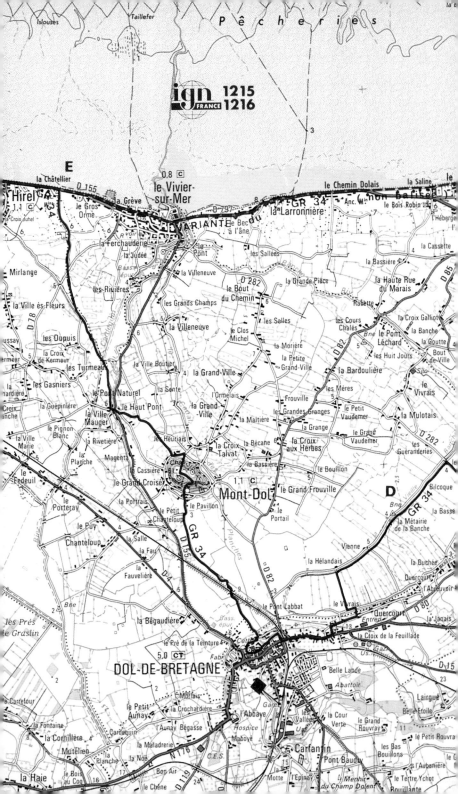

3Km
1:0

Detours, *There are several short walks in the area: 1) Walk round Saint-Marcan (1 hour) marked in white on signposts; 2) Walk around the surrounding area, through small wood on the plateau (3 hours) signposted in yellow; 3) Walk through surrounding grasslands (3 hours 30 mins) signposted in orange.*

SAINT-BROLADRE

Sculptured cross in the cemetery; old houses. On your left, is the Les Homeaux manor house with its beautiful portal.

11Km
2:45

model version of the 'original', which has been constructed by a local artist. The GR skirts a small pond, and then follows a dirt track to road edged here and there with shale outcrops and which looks down on Saint-Broladre. Pass through the hamlet of Les Muriaux and follow the road to a pond where you turn right (north) along a small path, which will take you the final meadow on your right. From here you have a good view over the bay and Saint-Joseph sanatorium, an elegant stone building. The GR drops down into an area of woods, ponds and waterfalls, and comes out at Saint-Broladre.

The GR runs alongside the Saint-Broladre cemetery, and then heads towards L'Orme, the outlying part of the town. Head left on the D80 for a few metres and then turn off left when you reach a bend to the right in the road, taking a path that runs between two barns. You will cross a private wood (access has kindly been granted to ramblers), cross a stream and then arrive at a road.

The GR passes through Le Tertre-Hubault, and thens runs alongside the ancient manor house of La Ville-Guillaume. Little of this is left now, only the ruined chapel beside the farm is still standing. Continue westwards along a paved lane then turn right (north), along a farm track. Turn left (west) at the first crossroads along a paved road which subsequently becomes tarmacadam. From this point, you have a superb view out over the marshes and the bay. After the cluster of houses at Vaujour, drop down right to the D80. Turn right along it, then take the second turning on the left, and make for Le Pont-au-Roux, which marks the beginning of the Dol Marshes. When you get to Le Pont-au-Roux, take the dirt track on your left. From here onwards the route follows a bridle path signposted in orange. You run alongside a canal, La Vieille Banche.

About 2 kilometres further on, you reach (but do not cross) a wooden bridge. Turn left (south), and take the path that runs alongside a field: make sure that you don't damage the crops or fences. The GR then dives down a tunnel underneath a busy road, and takes a

road westwards to the outskirts of Dol. It makes for the town centre.

DOL-DE-BRETAGNE

⌂ 𝗔 ✕ 🚉 🚌

Saint-Samson, a 13th century cathedral, well known for its size, two sculptured porches and large 14th century stained glass window. In the Middle Ages, the faithful would make a great 'Tro Breiz' (tour of Brittany) which took in all the holy places, Saint-Samson was one of these.

2Km
0:30

In Dol town, the GR turns right after the railway bridge and follows the Promenade des Douves (Dove Walk). It goes along a shopping street, and then follows a quaint tarmac street with old houses on each side to Saint-Samson cathedral.

The GR then drops down to the left (north) towards the marshes and takes a winding road to the village of Mont-Dol.

MONT-DOL

⌂ ✕ 🍷 🚉

Like Mont-Saint-Michel, Mont-Dol is a small granite island surrounded by legends of St. Michael's struggle with the Devil. Today it is no more than a headland which stands out against the surrounding area.
Palaeolithic flints and remains have been found here, and a sacrificial altar from a temple of Diana.

5Km
1:15

The GR34 takes the road through the village and then takes a sharp bend up towards the top of Mont-Dol. You will pass magnificent chestnut trees on this part of the walk, and a superb view awaits you at the top. Keep slightly left of the road, and make your way across the grasslands, ensuring that all gates are firmly closed. Drop down a steep path towards the north-west, and follow a series of small roads, some paved and some tarmac, across the marshes and canals to the coast and the tiny hamlet of La Châtellier on the D155.

La Châtellier

From La Châtellier there is an unmarked alternative route, which leads right (east) to Vivier-sur-Mer and Cherrueix, and rejoins the GR34 at an intersection of several dykes just after Chapelle de Sainte-Anne. (See dotted line on the map.)
From La Châtellier, the GR34 takes the D155 left to Hirel.

HIREL

𝗔 🚉 🚌

4Km
1:0

The GR34 continues west along the coast, following the D155 through Vildé-le-Marine and Saint-Benoît-des-Ondes.

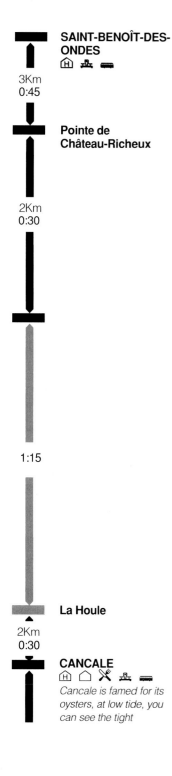

SAINT-BENOÎT-DES-ONDES
🏠 ⚓ 🚌

3Km
0:45

Pointe de Château-Richeux

2Km
0:30

1:15

La Houle

2Km
0:30

CANCALE
🏠 ⌂ ✕ ⚓ 🚌
Cancale is famed for its oysters, at low tide, you can see the tight

As you leave Saint-Benoît, you should turn left off the D155 and follow a path north-west which runs parallel to the road. The GR then cuts back across the D155 and follows the coastline again to La Pointe de Château Richeux.

From here onwards, the GR follows a new path which skirts the houses and overlooks the shore. This is the pedestrian footpath along the coast and is sign posted by a green arrow. Further on, when you come to a property surrounded by walls, follow the GR as it drops down onto the beach. Shortly afterwards you leave the shore and take the narrow passage running between two walls. Follow a dirt track which runs in front of Vaulerat Château — this takes you to a narrow one-way road. (The alternative GR34a route starts here.)

Alternative route (GR34a) Terrelabouët to Plage du Guesclin.
This signposted alternative route cuts 9 kilometres off the GR34 walk, rejoining it at Plage du Guesclin and makes a circular trip of 22 kilometres around Cancale.

The itinerary traces the steps of the old 'Parishioners' Walk' which was the route taken by processions from Cancale to Chapellle du Verger (Orchard Chapel).Go left past Terrelabouët on the narrow road described above, cut across the D76, and then follow a series of dirt tracks north, which run alongside fields where early vegetables are grown. Cross the D355, skirt round a valley and then plunge into a private wooded dell. Cross the D201 and you will then find yourself at Plage du Guesclin, where you meet up with the GR34.

The GR follows the narrow road to La Houle, which is a small fishing port on the outskirts of Cancale.

The GR runs alongside the port until it comes to the north jetty. A monument with a plaque marks the beginning of the *chemin de ronde* (footpath) which heads off up a paved lane. It follows the footpath over undulating

Pointe
du Grouin

Herp...
128

Chenal de la Vieille Rivière

Île des L...

la Foi

38

Pointe
du Nid

Pointe
de la Moulière

P. des Saussayes

33

le Haut
Bout

Bne

44

Camp

Chât.

Port-Mer

Gran

de (

Vez

Fort du Guesclin

G

Bne

40

le Verger

Plage du Verger

le Valade

la Ville
Blanche

Basse

Anc.
min

Pointe
du Chatry

Plage du Guesclin

GR 34

Chap.
la Gaudichais

41

la Cergnais

D 201

la Pintelais

la
Baie

Port-Briac

la Margot

la Ville
Hernier

Chât.

la Motte

47

Tannée

la Douve

la Ville
Auray

la Mettrie Fourdoré

35

la Ville Gueurie

St-Jouan

la Ville
ès-Péniaux

les Vaux

Pointe
de la Chaîne

36

Roch
de Can

le Champ
Lévier

la Forêt

D 355

4

la Motte Jean

Quatrevais

Atel.

Chât.
d'eau

la Verrie

50

la Broustière

1,6 C

St-Coulomb

le Bas Bois

la Ville-ès-Gris

la Ville Jégu

Chât.
d'eau

39

la V.
Garnier

29

Cancale

40

les Landes

Bne

52

la Croix
Blanche

46

les Boulais

le Bois
du Père

la Vieuville

St
épur.

D 76

D 201

D 276

Pisc.

4,8 CT

Tlle

la Ville
Poulet

le Plessis Bertrand
(Vest.)

la Houle

Parcs à huîtres

la Ville
Hersent

Terrelabouet

le Tertre
Janson

56

Min.

Pointe
des Roches Noires

Champ d'Avoine

le Flachet

le Pont

la Motte-Souris

Thion

39

les Bougras

29

Anc. min

le Vauléraut

les Petites
Landes

55

D 74

la Croix
de l'Orme

la Lignerie

49

D 76

Beauregard
Ch...

le Grand Porcon

Hôtellerie

le Domaine
Robin

43

les Portes
Rouges

la Coudre

GR 34

Ondes

les Ouches-
Boeufs

H... Ville

41

40

la Loirie

la
St
épur.

Ch... de
la Moussaye

Ch... Richeux

Pyl.

le Buot

F

Anc. min

la Couaillerie

8

Bassins

48

le Vaupinel

9

Anc...

latticework of the oyster beds. Also the home of the Amis des Chemins de Ronde (Friends of the Footpath Association), which is trying to rescue and restore the coastal footpaths.

8Km
2:0

countryside, and you may find that the tracks are sometimes difficult to find as there are insufficient props for signposts. Make sure that you don't take one of the numerous paths which lead down to the beach by mistake. When you come to the rather gloomy Rocher de Cancale and the fortified Île de Cancale the GR skirts an estate. Be careful if you are coming from the opposite direction, as you may not notice the change of direction. The GR then crosses several small marinas until it comes to the beach at Port-Mer, where you will find restaurants and cafés. Follow the sea-front for about 100 metres and then head off again along the footpath. You will pass a campsite and then come to the start of La Pointe du Grouin in front of the houses. If you go out onto the point, return here to continue the walk.

POINTE DU GROUIN

You can walk out to the tip of the point along the small paths through the gorse. This is a wild location, especially when the sea is rough, but views of the surrounding area are superb.

The GR follows the coastline westwards, initially along paths overgrown with gorse where signposts may be infrequent, and then along a recently made track. Drop down to Plage des Saussayes and go along the shore. Cross a stream and climb up to the right beside a fence. You join the coastal footpath, which heads round La Pointe de la Moulière with its old fortress, and then runs alongside Plage du Verger (Orchard Beach). Then take the road south-west to Chapelle du Verger.

5Km
1:30

From La Pointe du Grouin to Saint-Malo and Dinan, the coastal footpath is the scene of a small battle: bit by bit the authorities are acquiring the land, helped by the bye-law governing right of way beside the sea. The GR is having to adapt as these coastguard footpaths are regained for use, and you will find that there will be frequent small changes to the route.

Chapelle du Verger

The sailors of Cancale used to make pilgrimages to this ancient chapel. Votive offerings on display.

At the chapel, the GR follows the coastal footpath again to the Dôles look-out tower. You should make your way round a campsite and then drop down into the pine trees until you come to a beach. At this point, take the

dirt track on your right. The GR circumnavigates the Pointe du Nid (Nest Point) along the coastal footpath. Follow the dyke down to Plage du Guesclin.

Plage du Guesclin
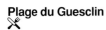

Alternative route GR34a. Plage du Guesclin to Terrelabouët (see page 51). Here you join up on your left with the GR34a alternative route (signposted) which makes a circular 22 kilometre walk round Cancale and rejoins the GR34 (past Terrelabouët) on the other side of the D76.

From here, work is in progress on the coastal footpath. It is passable, but parts are still overgrown.

The GR34 runs along Plage du Guesclin on the sand below the dyke.

Take great care on the cliff edge!

Beside a small house at the western tip of Plage du Guesclin, the GR ventures onto La Pointe des Grands-Nez (Big Noses Point). If the going on the point becomes too difficult, retrace your steps and then head right alongside the field towards a thicket — this is private land, and there are few signposts.

7Km
2

Roz-Ven
Novelist Colette lived here and her story Le Blé en Herbe *(The Ripening Seed) is based here.*

At Roz-Ven (see left) you have two options: 1) at high tide , you can follow the marked route which heads south round La Touesse beach along the D201. On your left, you will see a small footpath (a 12 kilometre walk), signposted with white circles, which leads to the château of La Ville-es-Offrans. (See dotted line on map); 2) at low tide, you can climb down across the rocks to Plage de Touesse and head round the rocky promontory (marked with a dotted line on the map). At the far end of Plage de la Touesse, the GR takes the coastal footpath to La Pointe du Meinga. Here, you should take the path through the gorse and then leave the coast to follow a route heading due south, which is used by the farm Les Nielles. You will subsequently come to La Guimorais.

LA GUIMORAIS

The GR takes a path on the right leading to Étang du Lupin, which is blocked off by a ruined dyke. This dyke may be under water, if so, cross over the dyke at the other end of the lake. Make your way along the muddy

coastline, which gradually becomes rocky then sandy as you approach Rotheneuf. This part of the route is difficult at high tide, as the sea covers part of the beach at Rotheneuf harbour. When the sea is in leave the beach and turn right onto the D201.

Detour, *(3 hours)*
La Ville-es-Offrans

2..5Km
0:40

From here you can detour and visit the 17th century château of La Ville -es-Offrans. Take the diversion which heads southwards and is signposted to the château. This continues after the château along a PR path, marked in white circles, and rejoins the GR at the south end of Plage de la Touesse. The whole circular detour is 12 kilometres long.

The GR follows either the road leading down to the beach or the D201 to Rothéneuf.

ROTHENEUF

4.5Km
1:10

The GR turns right at the first street in Rothéneuf, and then runs alongside a field in front of an estate. It leads to the chapel at Notre-Dame-des-Flots (Our Lady of the Waves). Ramblers coming from the opposite direction (west) can, at this point, assess whether the level of the tide will enable them to proceed along Rothéneuf beach and to the Étang du Lupin. You should pass the entrance to the Rochers Sculptées (rocks sculpted by Abbé Fouré) and rejoin the beach at Plage du Val, where the route follows a bridle path. Continue along the road and dirt tracks to La Pointe de la Varde and skirt this stretch of former military territory. The GR arrives at Le Pont at the north-east tip of the beach.

Le Pont

5Km
1:15

The markings lead you along the road running parallel to the coast, but you can walk along beside the sea all the way to Saint-Malo, tide permitting (links between the road and the beach are signposted), or you can take a bus all the way to the old corsair town.

SAINT-MALO

Old walled town ravaged in World War II, but reconstruction has preserved much of its character. Views of the

The best way to cross the Rance estuary so that you can rejoin the GR34 at Dinard, is to take the 10 minute boat trip across. This service is seasonal. You will get excellent views of the estuary, the ramparts of Saint-Malo and the old city fortress. Catch the boat at the south side of the walled town. Full details of the service at the harbour station at Saint-Malo.

town, the River Rance and the surrounding ports from ramparts: tomb of the French writer Châteaubriand on the little island of Le Grand Bé, accessible at low tide.

Whenever possible, an alternative route will be given, but more detailed information is available at the dam itself.

0:10

Alternative route Saint-Malo to ferry station at Dinard across the Barrage de la Rance. If you want to walk across, follow the unmarked GR to the *barrage* (dam) over the Rance. (You can cut considerable time off the journey by catching a local bus at Saint-Servan to Rosais hospital.) In Saint-Malo, follow the locks and the ferry car park to Saint-Servan beach and then take the pleasant coach road to the Promenade du Fort d'Aleth. Continue past Tour Solidor, skirt the quays and then turn into a street underneath an arch. At low tide, you can turn right, across the public gardens, and go down a flight of steps onto the shore — but be careful if the tide is coming in. At high tide, you can make your way round Sainte-Croix church and follow the little streets to Rosais beach. From the beach, a pleasant coastal footpath leads to the dam, and you cross it on a footbridge. You join up with the GR34c on the other side. If you now head north, you will take about 1.5 hours to reach Dinard. You rejoin the GR34 at the ferry.

DINARD

🏠 ⛺ 🍴 ⚓ 🍴

Boat trips in the summer to Saint-Malo

The GR34c heads south along the Promenade du Clair de Lune. You will first pass closeby to the aquarium and Sea Museum, then the small marina (there is a car park at the Quai de la Perle) and then, after walking along below some rather magnificent villas, you will come to the Plage du Prieuré beside a swimming-pool. Make your way along the beach and look out for a rather difficult pathway at the other end: if the going is too tough, you can always make a loop round the road.

PLAGE DU PRIEURÉ

Head inland and make your way round a walled estate. You will pick up a coastguard footpath which is maintained by the Amis des Chemins de Ronde (Friends of the Footpath Association): the path heads round La Pointe

59

de la Vicomté through a wooded area, which is more enjoyable at high tide, and there is a wide view out over the estuary, the city fortress and Solidor de Saint-Servan tower. Bizeux rock is in the foreground, with a statue of the Virgin Mary on top. When you get to La Vicomté, the path heads south and brings you out at the Rance tidal power station dam. Near to a small creek (Le Pissot), the track heads inland and makes its way past the beautiful Château de la Vicomté, which is now a holiday centre. The route continues over a housing estate, and then comes to the departure point for the electric cables carrying the current produced by the power station.

You should now follow the EDF route down to the beginning of the Rance dam.

5Km
1:30

Detour,
100m to the west
♒

Barrage de la Rance
The dam is 700 metres long and is home to a nuclear power station, the first of its type in the world. You can visit any day of the week.

2Km
0:30

The walker is affected by the dam, in that the times of high tide around it are impossible to forecast; what is more, there are several parts of the route which are only passable if the tide isn't too far in.

LA RICHARDAIS
⌂ Å ✕ ⚓
In the church, there are stained-glass windows and modern frescos.

Head south away from the dam along a dirt track, where there is a good view of the whole structure from the public gardens. You should then make your way across the shipyard, remaining outside the fence. After a rocky patch, you will come out below the D114 road. The descent to a small beach is sometimes impossible at high tide, in which case you should make your way round the slope and then the access road leading to the Grognet gardens. Go down from these gardens towards the small port of La Richardais, and then follow the road leading to the market town.

Go down the main road to a bridge: the wooden staircase on your left will lead to a narrow path beside the water, and you should make your way round the bottom of the creek. Just to the right of the restaurant, you will notice a small door in a wall, which leads to the path round the Pointe de Cancaval. Make your way along this magnificent path and you will meet a small road leading away from the point. Turn off to the left, between the houses.

Alternative route to the Moisiais. Continue to the right of the mouth of a stream, and pick up the coastal footpath. After a wooded hillock, follow the road along beside Jouvente dock, where you rejoin the Moisiais.

You will come to a small mooring area, where you may find that a wall which drops down into the water is blocking your passage at high tide. If this is the case, you will have to climb up and follow the gravel road at the top, and then take the second road on the left. You will then find a path which goes back down to the coast (the signpost has been put there by the Friends of the Footpath Association). From Gauthier beach, take the lane round Les Hures, which will take you on to the tiny hamlet of La Landriais.

LA LANDRIAIS

Go down on to the shore. If the steps are under water, you will have to scale the wall a bit higher (handholds are difficult to find) or alternatively you can go round via Trégondé: two left turns will bring you out on the coast close to a white house with a sign saying `Cafe-Restaurant du Port'. Cross over the shipyard – it may be damp under foot at high tide – and then turn off the road to the left. The entrance to the yard is rather hidden, to the left of some wire fencing, but the exit is well marked with steps and a signpost. A dirt track leads over a building plot, and you should then head along La Gréve du Marais (or Garel) for a few metres before climbing down the steps. Another dirt track will now lead past a hospice, close to Minihic-sur-Rance.

3Km

MINIHIC-SUR-RANCE

There is a 7 kilometre PR route which follows the GR and returns to the town via narrow grassy tracks: this takes 2 hours.

The dirt track joins up with the coast again, and you soon come to an old ruined sea mill. The dyke belonging to the mill can be crossed at low tide; at other times, you will have to go round the bottom of the creek. The next dyke, which the GR then follows, can be crossed at all times. Make your way round La Pointe de Trégondais along the shore, and then walk along Morlet beach. When you come to a chapel, the path heads inland. The town of Saint-Suliac is on the other bank. As you climb back up the cliff, you will pass two towers, which are not marked very clearly. Then head through a small wood to Langrolay.

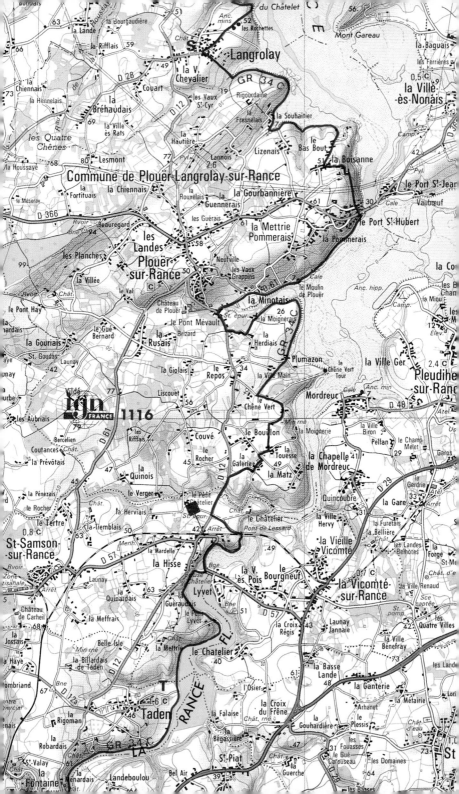

LANGROLAY

5Km
1:30

PORT-SAINT-HUBERT

The bridge was destroyed in the war, but was then rebuilt in 1959. The central arch spans 175 metres.

PLOUËR HARBOUR

Detour, *15 mins,*
PLOUËR-SUR-RANCE

5Km
1:30

Turn left when you reach the market town and go down a dirt track to a stream. Then head back towards the coast, and make your way along it to the outlying houses of Le Souhaitier (the path runs along the muddy shore). Cross over the road near to the chapel, and then descend into the small wood on your left to pick up the shore in an easterly direction. Make sure you do not miss the small road leading to the beach, which starts between a low wall and the ruins of an old wall. Turn left when you come to the hamlet of La Boisanne, then right just before a big door, along a lane which becomes very narrow.

From Port-Saint-Hubert, you should make for the coast and cross under the suspension bridge over the Rance. Continue along the lane and then over the shore and rocks, until you get to the harbour of Plouër.

You may find that an old sea mill dyke stops you getting through: if this happens, you will have to make a large detour via the bottom of the creek to get to the other side of the dyke. It is sometimes very muddy after La Moignerais.

Make your way along the shore again in a southerly direction. Turn inland when you get to the south-east corner, along a small road, and then follow a dirt track which becomes a very sunken lane. Go down through Chêne-Vert wood, and then climb up to the right to make your way through a small hamlet.

If you are coming in the opposite direction, look out for a narrow passage between two houses and then take the path on the left which climbs up towards the woods.

A series of dirt tracks and small roads will bring you out on the D12, where you should turn left in a southerly direction. As you approach the access road leading to a château, turn left and then descend to the right towards the Rance: make your way underneath the railway viaduct and then join up with the towpath again.

**Écluse du Chatelier
(lock-gates)**

This marks the edge of the Rance basin and the start of the canalised section. First pass the lock controls, then follow the towpath along to Dinan. The Rance is still broad in parts and the path, which winds and has steep banks, provides a pleasant walk.

The path rejoins the main route at

DINAN

*Picturesque old town.
Fortifications. Clock tower.*

WALK 3

RENNES
(See p.19)

Detour,
Château de Fontenay. Fontenay, to the north of Chartres-de-Bretagne, was where Henri IV, Louis XIII, and other Kings of France stayed several times. There is now a farm on the site of the château, and a chapel with some parts dating from the 13th, 14th and 16th centuries.

6.5Km
1:30

In Rennes, the route begins at the West gate (L'Entrée Ouest) of the Parc de Brequigny. Alternatively you can join it later by taking a bus to the 'Alma' shopping centre.

However, as the route is not very pleasant, you may prefer to take bus (12) to Chartres and pick up the GR there.

CHARTRES-DE-BRETAGNE
⌂ ✕ ⚲ ⚱ ▭
Formerly owned by the Château of Fontenay, Chartres was for a long time a flourishing pottery centre. A rare limestone formation has been found in the region, and disused lime kilns are open to visitors (west of the N137 road). Citroen factory.

3Km
0:45

The GR39 crosses the Place de l'Auditoire. Near the bus stop, take the Rue de Fénidian and then the Impasse de Fénidan. A pedestrian path leads close by a chapel.

Detour, *4 km*
Circular walk: Turn left in front of this chapel along the Rue Antoine Chatel, then the hamlet of Champ Rond, returning to the GR near the Château de Fontenay (see map opposite)

Continue heading south on a small road, then turn right to cross some playing fields. Further dirt tracks lead to La Chaussairie.

LA CHAUSSAIRIE
✕ ⚲ ⚱ ▭

The GR crosses the N137, then turns left.

Detour, *1hr*
BRUZ
✕ ⚱ ▭ ▥
The approach from La

Bearing south, the GR crosses the Bruz-La Chaussairie road. Take the gravel path heading west to the hamlet of Boutoir, go past the

69

Chaussairie to this sprawling market town is the nearest way to the station, along very attractive dirt tracks.

9Km
2:30

LE BOËL
✂ 🍷

Le Boël has a natural setting, in a small valley hollowed out by the River Vilaine. A lock; a well restored mill, dated 1662; countryside of cliffs and moors. (Not shown on map but see Ref. C)

4Km
1

Fénicat Pony Club until you reach a small bridge across the River Seiche. Turn right before the bridge, on a footpath for anglers: this is across private land, so do not disturb the ponies and close the gates with care. The footpath leads to a road. Cross the bridge and continue along the left bank to a private clinic, also on private land. Do not disturb anyone. Cross the car park, pass to the left of the buildings, through a gate and across a lawn; the way out is across a wooden bridge on the left. Continue, right, beside the river on a small road to a bridge over the Seiche. (Cross the bridge for the road leading into Bruz.) Take the small road to the hamlet of La Vigne, where the dirt track becomes a narrow footpath. At Le Dégage take the road to the right, and then at La Porte turn uphill on a track heading south. There is a complete change of scenery here, to moorland with furze and rocky outcrops. After two road crossings, descend slightly to Les Landelles, then bear west. A straight path runs beside the railway line, then turns left into Le Boël.

There are several walks in the area: 1. the hollows on the left bank are already very well used, while those opposite, on the right bank, are much quieter, although equally well supplied with footpaths; 2. the towpath leads north to Pont-Réan, 2.5 kilometres away on the Rennes-Redon road; and 3 kilometres to the south is Laillé, with a railway halt; 3. also on the right is the 9 kilometre circular walk (indicated with white markings) from Le Boël to the Sources (springs) de Bagatz. The railway halt at Laillé is also accessible from this circular walk, as well as the GR at the hamlet of Les Vallées, with a route back to Le Boël.

The GR stays on the left bank. Climb up to the top of the cliff which dominates the site, by a big track to the left of a quarry. There are successive viewpoints separated by small bushy hollows. Beyond the final view over the mill the GR comes to the fence at the back of the military terrain, Le CELAR, and continues for 1 kilometre between this fence and the Saint-Jean wood. Access to the wood is strictly forbidden and walkers should not linger on this stretch of the GR. This `corridor'

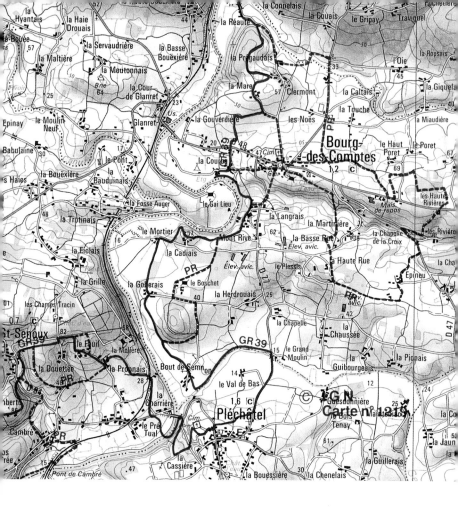

comes out beside a track leading into the wood; cross this to join a small public footpath running parallel to it. Do not use the forest track or go into the wood. On coming level with the CELAR buildings, turn right on a broad dirt track. At a small road the GR meets the footpath of the PR from Laillé, marked in orange and green. Beyond La Bouchetière the track goes down to the Vilaine valley, reaching the D39 at Les Vallées.

D39
Detour, *500m*
LA HALTE DE LAILLÉ
✕ 🍷 ⛽

Follow the D39 down to the River Vilaine.

Turning up the D39, the GR turns right behind a transformer. Bear left round the hamlet of Le Hyaume.

Detour, *1.5km*
LAILLÉ
♀ ⚒

This can be reached on a good track running from east to west.

5Km
1:15

Opposite the disused Bénioc quarry there is a particularly interesting geological fault line, clearly visible between Armorican Clay on the right and Congrier on the left.

La Réauté
This manor house, surrounded by high walls, still has a large tower, small square pavilion, and chapel (1700), with gun embrasures. Small portions of the old outer walls remain, including the 1503 gatehouse.

3Km
0:45

BOURG-DES-COMPTES
⌂ ⚔ ✕ ♀ ⚒
🚌 🅱

This is a district with varied scenery, three circular walks and more than a dozen manor houses. The small town itself has several very old houses, including the 15th century Manoir des Provostières.

7.5Km
2

LA COURBE
⚔ ♀ ⚒
Old houses and a chapel.

The GR soon reaches the edge of a valley; go down into it on a poor track beside a field, taking care not to walk on the crops. Other tracks, in better condition, cross the valley, by the Étang du Donhu and La Macillais. There is a wood at the top of the opposite slope; go round it to the right, with La Corbinais on the right, likewise the quarries by the Vilaine.

The GR continues down to the manor of La Réauté.

Take a small road and then a steep-sided track up through a pine wood to a hillock. Turn left towards the hamlet of Clermont, then turn back to the right to La Mare, from where Bourg-des-Comptes is visible. Take the track to the right and then to the left, which is slightly hollowed out, without waymarkings, cross a stream, then join the D48 road near Bourg-des-Comptes.

The GR crosses the D48 and continues straight on to the hamlet of La Courbe, on the edge of the Vilaine.

The GR, together with the 9 kilometre Boschet circular walk, marked in red, slips between a wall and the River Vilaine to the mill of La Courbe. A fine track goes round the walls of the Mont Rive estate; the drive to the château is on the right. The GR rises to 50 metres above the Vilaine; care is needed in following the marked track, which bears right off the main track several times at this viewpoint and is not very clear. From Le Mortier a track to the south leads to La Gohérais. To the east, note the Château du Boschet (see page 76). Turn right in the hamlet; the red signs for the

Le Château du Boschet

Rebuilt in the 17th century, the château consists of an enormous central building with a high mansard roof, flanked by four small curving pavilions. The chapel also dates from the 17th century. The château has vast and beautiful outbuildings and classic French gardens.

PLÉCHÂTEL

✗ ⚓ 🚐

One of the oldest towns in the area, Ploucastellum became Ploucastel in 1086, then Plouchatel - meaning the `parish of the château'. In the town there is a very fine calvary made from a single stone, with a four-sided roof and its base carved in the 15th century. Pléchâtel is famous for its `Levée', a schist cliff with caves, steps and small chapels carved out of it.

5.5Km
1:30

SAINT-SENOUX

🍷 ⚓

This little town has a strange Byzantine-style church established by a 19th century curé inspired by a pilgrimage to the Holy Land. Saint-Senoux, which is heavily wooded and has many valleys, is particularly well known for its network of footpaths; there are a dozen circular walks or links of varying length covering the district, all the little pathways being very well maintained.

6Km
1:30

Boschet circular walk appear shortly afterwards, leading off to the left. Next there is the hamlet of Bout-de-Semnon on the right; pass along the edge of a field to the River Semnon, a substantial tributary of the Vilaine. Go up-river, first on an anglers' path and then by the side of a field. Cross the Semnon at the bridge on the D77 and keep to this road. Turn right beside a sewage filter station, cross a field, or go round the edge if there are growing crops, to the small town of Pléchâtel.

The GR passes the walls of the monastery then winds through the steep outcrops of La Levée. To the north-east the Château of La Molière is visible. Cross the valley and go up on to heathland above the Vilaine, by the Croix des Jeunes Gens (the Young People's Cross). Go down again (north) to a bridge. Cross the bridge, noting the Semnon confluence on the right; go down to the tow path and follow it southwards. Under the bridge there is a plaque indicating the flood level in 1936. After 300 metres leave the river's edge, cross the road close to Saint-Senoux station, and continue towards the château of La Molière. The path passes below the château, then crosses La Pronais. Turn right in front of the farm, go past Le Feuil, then join a small road lined with very old oak trees. A footpath through the wood leads down to the small town of Saint-Senoux.

The GR continues through the wood, following the Fromiette stream. Cross the stream fairly soon, and go up a wooded hillside to the hamlet of Cambertu. Leave it on its access road and turn left to La Picardière. Carry on down into a valley, ford the stream, and go up again to Bruzon. From the next descent there is a broad view over the Vilaine valley and the Cambré bridge. Go down, right, through another wooded valley. This is private property, so take care during the hunting season. The footpath comes out close to the Vilaine; go steeply up again to the right. This old pilgrim track goes up to the Montserrat chapel, tucked into the woods on the left.

Montserrat chapel
*Fine Breton belfry dated
1879. A small road leads to
Saint-Malo-de-Phily.*

SAINT-MALO-DE-PHILY
♈ ⚓

*Old manor house with a
farm wagon decorated with
an upturned scallop shell
and two Renaissance
pilasters; a very large
church with a fine fresco;
panoramic view over the
Vilaine and the Rocher
(rock) d'Uzel.*

1Km
0:15

LA GARE DE PLÉCHÂTEL
⌂ ✕ ♈ ⚓ ▦

9.5Km
2:30

Plessix-Bardoult
*Home for former members
of the armed forces.
Walkers have permission to
cross the land, which they
should do with care.
During the 19th century an
iron works was set up here
near the pools, but with
competition from coke-fired
furnaces it was forced to
close.*

Detour, *2.5hrs*
BAIN DE BRETAGNE
⌂ ⛺ ✕ ⚓ ▦

Follow the small track down beside the sand quarries. A loop to the left goes close to the very large Montserrat quarries. Cross the Vilaine at La Gare de Pléchâtel.

The GR turns left beyond the bridge then right on to a steep wooded slope, the Rocher d'Uzel; climb the bulky rocks overlooking the valley. A footpath crosses the wood heading east; this is private land, so do not leave the marked track. Carry on by the edge of the wood round some fields, then turn south again on agricultural tracks to La Hamonnais. A narrow track comes out into the yard at La Préchetais farm. (In the opposite direction the GR goes out at the end of the yard, behind an old oven.) Carry straight on down the edge of the field; going through La Corvaiserie, there is a wide view over the estate of Le Plessix-Bardoult, which the GR also crosses.

Go past the pools and then, on a level with the main building, turn into a large avenue heading east. The GR goes close to the hamlet of L'Aubaudais, then takes a farm track opposite the Plessix-Bardoult avenue. This track crosses Les Landes de Bagaron, then turns right on to a road. Continue in a generally south-west direction, on large tracks; beyond La Héraudière, after a rather overgrown stretch, there is a wide view over the Vilaine. Turn left towards a pinewood, then two clearly visible hummocks known as `les Fesses de Gargantua'(Gargantua's bottom)! An attractive path leads down to the lower ground round Messac.

The GR takes a road to the right, while a local footpath, marked in white and yellow, continues

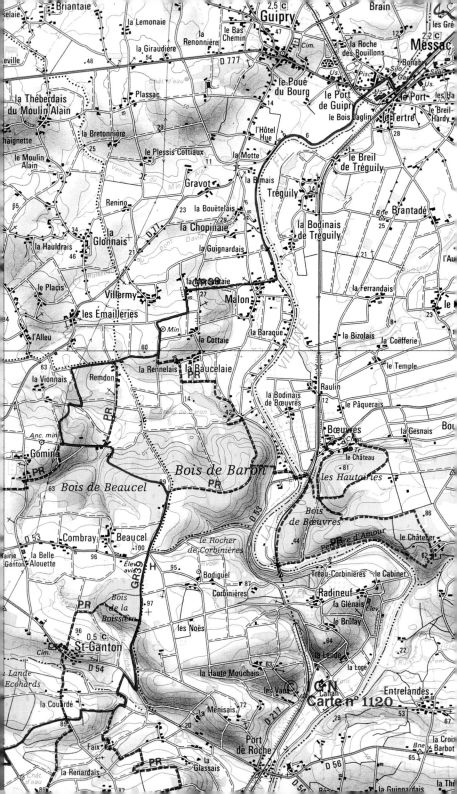

On the way down, take the PR footpath to the left, marked in white and blue.

MESSAC
🏠 △ ✕ 🚐 🅱

Les Corbinières
On its way out of the Messac basin the Vilaine has carved out a deep valley through the Corbinières land mass. the river is crossed by the Saint-Marc road bridge and by the railway on a remarkable viaduct followed by a tunnel.

LE PORT DE GUIPRY
🏠 🛖 ✕ 🍸

Le Port de Guipry, on the other side of the Vilaine, consists of old buildings, some of which were used as salt stores. The charming chapel of Notre Dame du Bon Port, dating from 1644, was built as the result of a vow when the Vilaine was in flood and threatening the salt store.

A small iron ore deposit was dug out at Les Forges about 100 years ago.

15Km
4

straight on. A fairly long stretch of road, then a disused railway line, leads to the edge of the Vilaine. Go through a small tunnel under the Rennes-Redon line. Carry on to the left on an increasingly narrow track between the railway embankment and the river. Take care not to slip in wet weather. After passing along the edge of a field the GR reaches the hamlet of Clédy. Go through the copse of Les Grées, where there are some standing stones, and then take the small road which leads to the market town of Messac.

There are several ways to explore this area: 1. there is a footpath through the wood on the right bank of the Vilaine, which can be combined with the towpath to make a small loop; 2. on the right bank, around the Moulin de Baron and the Étang de Baron, are four circular walks, of between 2 and 7 kilometres, whose footpaths cross the wooded hillsides on good paved tracks; 3. in the Boeuvres hill on the left bank, with access by the Saint-Marc bridge and a small tunnel under the railway line, there is another network of narrower footpaths; 4. the circular walk of L'Hermitage, marked in blue, offers fine views from the cliffs over the Vilaine, the loop in the river, the marshes on the left bank and the viaduct.

The GR crosses the Vilaine, then turns left on the towpath, the only way to cross this agricultural area. After 4 kilometres leave the riverbank at the Malon lock and go up a small road towards La Mordantaie, then the mill at Les Bruyères, where there is rising land and wide views. To the south, Étang de Baron lies below a wooded hill, to be climbed shortly. The GR makes a fairly wide bend towards more high ground to the west, with some small valleys first, following roughly the route of a major electricity line. Shortly before reaching the ruins of the mill of La Tombe, go down to the left towards the hamlet of Les Forges.

Turn right by the bank of a pool, then on the right follow a footpath beside a smaller electricity line. This stretch has been kindly authorised by the landowners: walkers are requested to be careful of growing crops and not to smoke. Leaving the electricity line on

Detour, *2.5km*
THE BARON POOL
♀

*Take the footpath with blue
indicator markings, which
has been following the
same route as the GR, to
the left.*

La Couarde

Detour, *10 mins,*
SAINT GANTON
⌂ ♀ ⚒

*Access by the small road
from the north. Three
circular walks, of 6, 8 and
24 kilometres leave Saint
Ganton, making use of part
of the GR, as well as a
footpath of a medium
distance walk linking Saint
Just to the massif de
Boeuvres.*

Detour, *1 hour,*
LANGON
✗ ⚒ ⚘

*Langon 12th/15th century
church, with a 12th century
fresco; the chapel of Sainte
Agathe, with its Roman
fresco; some thirty
standing stones, known as
`les Demoiselles de
Langon'; a network of
footpaths, with good tracks
across the heath.*

9Km
2:15

the right, go round a meadow to Le Foutet, a small manor house surrounded by fine trees.

The access road to Le Foutet meets up with the D53; cross it and go along the dirt track opposite, lined with furze bushes. The track passes the edge of the wood to a small valley. Turn up right on the D54, then turn left and left again on good gravel paths, which lead up to the hamlet of La Couarde.

Detour (see left). Take the road to the left (south), and carry straight on at each crossroads. When the gravel path which succeeds it meets a cross track, turn left. the small valley there goes down to the station. The town is 1 kilometre to the south of the station, and can be reached by continuing straight on along the track heading east-south-east above the valley.

From La Couarde, the GR continues heading west on a good gravel path and meets the D59 opposite a tarred track. Turn left on the D59 for about 100 metres, then turn on to a dirt track to the right, which goes south round the wooded estate of Le Bot. Turn right on to a small road, and carry straight on where it turns left. Turn right on the first track thereafter, between the wood and a field, where the markings are difficult to find. Carry on steadily to the north along a straight but varied track.

All this stretch of the GR is across private land, and is permitted on condition that walkers behave quietly and sensibly. Do not smoke. There is a break in the track on a level with the Grande Vallée farm; go along the edge of a field, continuing in the same line as the track. Slightly further on, both before and after passing the Suénay farm, keep off any freshly planted ground. Turn left on to a gravel path and leave it again to the left just before reaching the houses at Le Mérienneuf; go down through very fine oak trees near a small pool covered with lilies. This marks the end of the stretch across private land.

La Chapelle de Gavrain

Chapel surrounded by slabs of stone forming an enclosure; old houses built of the schist typical of the Redon area.

Turn up to the west on a gravel path to a small road, and turn left along it, then turn right in to the wood. Here the GR follows the track of a PR path, marked in yellow. Follow this path to the left for 1 kilometre to the hamlet of La Chapelle de Gavrain. The track through the wood, the Chemin des Panages, carries on for some distance to the west, straight but undulating and wooded. It leads to the D177 road.

Junction with the D177
(from Rennes to Redon)

Follow this very busy road for 200 metres, then turn right on to a gravel path. Opposite a fairly wide track on the left, turn right along the edge of the wood. Here the GR leaves the yellow markings of the PR walk.

Detour, *2.5km,*
Launay Hingan
A remarkable place built entirely of schist.
Continue on the PR path.

4Km
1

Detour, *4.5km,*
Renac
If you continue on the PR walk, this is a substantial short-cut to Redon.

The path along the wood continues to the left on an unmarked track, while the GR is to the right (north), towards Saint-Just. Reach the town on a gravel path through the hamlet of Bresquemin, a small valley full of furze then a road.

SAINT-JUST
△ 🏕 ✕ 🍷 ⚓

The importance of Saint-Just as a megalithic site places it second only to

Leave the small town on the lane to the campsite, and turn right there towards a mill and then left towards a line of standing stones. The dirt track continues to the left of a house; continue on the succeeding good gravel

9Km
2:15

Carnac in the whole of France. There are numerous prehistoric structures scattered around, in particular on the Lande de Cojoux, which is crossed by the GR:
1) The Moulin Lines, excavated and restored: 13 large blocks of quartzite, orientated east-west; 20 metres to the south there is another line of schist and quartzite stones crossing a tumulus, and another line further to the south. Traces of wooden structures have been found which were used to raise or prop up the stones. ̄
2) The Demoiselles de Cojoux: 2 magnificent quartzite standing stones, with a third lying down.
3) The tumulus of Château-Bu, with 8 blocks of quartzite on top arranged in a circle, making a megalithic tomb `Le Tribunal'.
4)The hillock of the Croix Saint-Pierre, made up of a rectangle of stones, schist on the north and quartzite on the south, with a standing stone at each corner.
5)The covered way, partly fallen in, of the Four Sarrazin.

path, with the Demoiselles de Cojoux on the right. Carry on along the track for about 100 metres, then turn off to the right towards the tumulus of Château-Bu. Go across the tumulus, carry on to a crossroads, and bear slightly left (west). After 200 metres there is another tumulus mound on the right, the Croix Saint-Pierre. The track turns right, and on the right there is the covered way of the Pierres Chevèches. The track continues to the Etang du Val, surrounded by rocks and woods, past the top of the rocks used for climbing. The tracks down used by climbers go to the right of the rocks, beside the pool. Walkers who are less robust will find a gently sloping footpath a little further to the right. The GR passes the foot of the tracks, then continues, very undulating, more or less close to the pool. At the retaining bank turn to the left of the buildings, then left again to the road. Cross Le Vieux Bourg on the right. Take a good track to the right across a hillside, which soon overlooks the Canut valley. Passing the Trohinat ford to the right, carry on across the heathland. At a sharp bend to the left, turn right to the edge of the Canut; shortly before a road bridge, go up to the left through bracken on the left bank of a small stream; this stretch may be difficult when the bracken is growing. Come out on to a gravel path. The GR turns right on to the gravel path, then immediately left. Go down to a road, and turn right off it to cross the Canut.

The `pallis', stone slab barriers

The 'pallis' are walls or barriers of slabs schist, characteristic of the Pays de Redon agricultural landscape. These slabs, of more or less regular shape, are put together either with bindings of chestnut branches - the oldest method, found in particular round Launay Hingant - or with planks of the same wood, or rails split lengthways, called 'limandes'. Pigs especially were kept in enclosures surrounded by strong fences of this type, firmly held together with broad beams.

Alternative route in winter the Gannedel Marsh. From December to May the marsh may be flooded for several days, following rainy periods. It is then impossible to follow the route from the Roche de Timouy. At such times follow the PR footpath to the right, leading to the small town of Sainte Marie, then back to the GR just before the slate quarry.

Château de la Haye

From the rise after the bridge across the Canut there is a fine view back over the château. Dating form 1620, it consists of a main building with a vast emblazoned pediment, wings flanked with high-roofed turrets and a moat. Most clearly visible are the corner towers with domed roofs.

3Km
0:45

Crossing of paths

7Km
1:45

You turn right in front of the houses at Le Bas Coipel. At a fork the footpath marked in blue goes off to the left, while the GR turns right along a fine long ridgeway through the wood, the Chemin du Carosse (the Carriage Track).

After 2.3 kilometres this very ancient track comes to the corner of a wood with a crossing of ways. To the right (north), following the main track, was the old GR39a, which is currently impassable. The GR39 turns left (south) on a rather overgrown path, and then joins a road. Turn left, then right on a large track with, at the end, the blue markings of the Palis circular walk. Turn right. The shared track goes through the hamlet of La Hilais, then at the bottom of a slope turns right on a small track. A farm track leads to the hamlet of Trobert. The Saint-Fiacre chapel is beside the path, in an attractive setting, close by a stream and a drinking water fountain. Cross the stream and go up opposite on a track through the wood. Pass the Launay Saint-Fiacre farm, to the left. The footpath goes down into the valley again, near the Faubuisson mill. Together with fresh yellow markings and still going through the wood, the GR comes to the back of the houses and the hamlet of Le Pont de Renac.

Le Pont de Renac

Detour, *20 mins,*
RENAC
⚑ ⚒

Keep to the Palis circular walk, with blue markings, which goes left in the hamlet of Le Pont de Renac.

4Km
1

The GR goes past the front of the houses, then down to the D177. There is a broad view left over the Gannedel marsh; look to see if it is flooded. Follow the main road for 200 metres, then turn left on a raised track. This meets another track, with, on the right the PR footpath, marked in yellow, to be used in case of floods.

The GR continues along a good track. Be careful not to miss the narrow footpath to the left across a meadow; the track curves to the

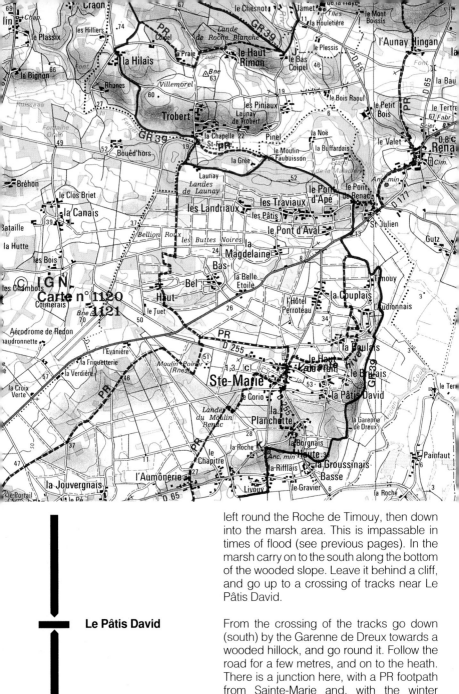

Le Pâtis David

left round the Roche de Timouy, then down into the marsh area. This is impassable in times of flood (see previous pages). In the marsh carry on to the south along the bottom of the wooded slope. Leave it behind a cliff, and go up to a crossing of tracks near Le Pâtis David.

From the crossing of the tracks go down (south) by the Garenne de Dreux towards a wooded hillock, and go round it. Follow the road for a few metres, and on to the heath. There is a junction here, with a PR footpath from Sainte-Marie and, with the winter alternative, is to be used when the marsh is flooded. Cross the former slate quarries on a hummocky track. Take the small road which

Detour, *15 mins,*
SAINTE-MARIE
✗ ♈ ⚏
Cross Le Pâtis David and
continue straight on.

5Km
1:15

LE CHAPITRE
♈ ⚏

L' AUMÔNERIE
♈

Pont du Grand Pas
Detour, *500m north*
LA CHÈVRE
♈ ⚏

6Km
1:30

Here the GR joins the
Grand Pas circular walk,
with blue markings.

runs along beside the waste dump and through a hamlet, then a big track on the right which passes a series of fields liable to flooding.
In case of difficulty, go back to the Sainte Marie-Redon road, cross Le Chapitre and L'Aumônerie.

Pick up the GR by taking a gravel path to the left just after a bridge - the track goes down the other side of the hill to the Fouy road. Beyond the Rohignac ruins, where there are the remains of a turret with steps, the GR joins a gravel path by the side of the marsh to Fouy.

Rejoin the towpath, go under the bridge and follow the edge of the Vilaine to the foot of a wooded hillside, La Ruche. Take the footpath, which zig-zags steeply up the slope through the pine trees, then bears left. The way down, which is less steep, goes past the deserted La Bonde farm, then back to the towpath again. Carry on along the path to the outskirts of Redon.

REDON

🏠 △ ⚊ ✕ ☉
⛟ ⛟ ⚊ 🅱

Redon is the capital of the Pays de Vilaine, is also at the crossroads of two navigable water channels, used increasingly by river tourists: the Vilaine, which after Rennes goes north as far as the Channel via the Ille canal and Rance; the Nantes-Brest canal, which the GR347 frequently runs alongside. From the gardens on both sides of the railway line there is a good view over the Vilaine valley and the apse of the Norman church of Saint-Sauveur. The 12th century belltower is the only one of its kind in Brittany. The choir is 13th century Gothic; A second 14th century bell tower, has a 67 metre high stone spire. Island of the port, with its 17th and 18th century shipowner's houses; Rue du Port, with its salt storehouses and old residences; old town: Grande-rue, Rue de la Monnaie, Rue d'Enfer and Rue Notre-Dame.

6Km
1:30

Detour, *15km,*
The Circuit du Grand Pas

A circular walk, marked in blue, which goes through the wooded hills on the left riverbank upstream from the town, crosses the marsh and the Vilaine at Pont du Grand Pas, and returns to Redon by the GR.

Redon is the meeting place for many footpaths: 1. the GR39, `Manche-Océan', coming from Mont-Saint-Michel and Rennes via the Vilaine valley, and proceeding to the south of Redon via La Roche-Bernard and La Brière as far as Guérande; 2. the GR of the `pays des Trois Rivières' (three-river country), looping for several days east of Redon via the Gavre forest and the valleys of the Don, the Chère and the Vilaine; 3. the GR38, heading west towards the moors of Lanvaux and the Montagnes Noires (Black Mountains) along ridges covered with pines and gorse; 4. the GR347, described below, which serves as a link between the GR38 and the GR37, going through the centre of Brittany in the heart of the Argoat.

Warning: Modifications of the GR347 are expected. Follow any new markings, always giving them priority over the description here.

SAINT-PERREUX-VIEUX-BOURG
✗ 𝖸 ⚓

4Km
1

This is eel-fishers' country. Take a look at the chapel in the old town and the view from the Roche du Theil.

Crossroads
Detour, *15 mins,*
SAINT-VINCENT-SUR-OUST
⌂ ✗ 𝖸 ⚓

1Km
0:15

At the crossroads, follow the road to the left.

TI-KENDAL'CH
⌂ ⛺

From here you can view the rocks for climbers on the île aux Pies (magpie island), one of the most beautiful sites of the Morbihan interior.

6Km
1:30

Go down to the right through the woods to meet the towpath, which you follow to the left. Climb up again to your left as far as the old quarries.

D138

5Km
1:15

Follow this road to the canal. Here the two GRs separate: the GR38 goes left (west) and the GR347 takes the D138 road straight ahead.

To the right you will see the Mortier (swamp) de Glénac, the domain of water-birds, which inspired Paul Féval's novel, *La Femme Blanche du Marais* (The White Lady of the Marsh).

SAINT-JACOB
𝖸

3:5Km
1

LES FOURGERÊTS
⛺ ✗ ⚓

4Km
1

Listed yew-tree near church.

Moulin du Vaulaurent
Near the mill and the Vaulaurent lagoon, you will find the chapel of Notre-Dame du Bon Accueil.

4Km
1

Detour, *30 mins,*
SAINT-MARTIN-SUR-OUST

Take the road to the right, then the second on the left to reach the far north of the lagoon. On

⌂ 人 ✕ ⵟ ⚖

*Follow the road to the left,
then go left again on the
D14.*

Les Gaudines de Haut
(See map ref. d)
Detour, *30 mins,*
CASTELLAN
⌂

4Km
1

*At the entrance to the
hamlet of Les Gaudines de
Haut, take a minor road on
the left for 1.5 kilometres,
then a path to the right
which leads to the Château
de Castellan.*

SAINT-CONGARD
✕ ⵟ ⚖

*House of Nominoë, the first
ruler of Brittany; cross in
the cemetery; stele near
the church; fence made of
little pointed stakes (east of
town); transverse valley of
Saint-Congard.*

10Km
2:30

MALESTROIT
⌂ ⌂ 人 ✕ ⵟ
⚖ 🚂

*A country holiday resort.
Church of Saint-Gilles, half
Romanesque, half Gothic;
old town with 15th and 16th
century houses; the cross
near the clinic; picturesque
bridges over the Oust and
the canal; remains of the
chapel of Saint-Michel,
where the Truce of
Malestroit was signed.*

6Km
1:30

SAINT-MARCEL
ⵟ ⚖

*Memorial to the fighting on
18 June 1944, after which
the whole town went up in
flames.*

5Km
1:15

the right you will find the markings for the
GR39a. Go left along the D14; 100 metres
further on, turn right and follow a long land
regroupment path. Take a road on the right,
then a forest path to the left to come out at a
minor road. You will come to the vicinity of Les
Gaudines de Haut.

**Crossroads with the
PR circular walks**
Detour, *1 hr*
SÉRENT
🏠 🏕 ✕ 🍷 🚃

9Km
2:15

*15th/16th century church;
cross, chapels and valley
of Tromeur.*

Go straight ahead in a westerly direction at
the crossroads of the GR and the PR.

**LE ROC-SAINT-
ANDRÉ**
🏠 🏕 ✕ 🍷 🚃

*18th century listed bridge
over the Oust.*

7Km
1:45

Detour, *500m*
to the right along the N166.
LA GARE
🏠 ✕

QUILY
🍷 🚃

6Km
1:30

SAINT-SERVANT
🍷 🚃

*Renaissance church;
calvary; old houses.*

At the centre of the town, the GR turns right,
passes to the left of the cemetery, turns right,
then left to meet the D122 via a land
regroupment path; follow the D122 to the
right to Saint-Gobrien.

2.5Km
0:40

SAINT-GOBRIEN
🍷

*14th century chapel; old
houses.*

CAHÉRAN
🍷 🚃

*Junction with the GR37
which comes on the right
(east) from Guillac and
Ploermel; to the left (west)
the GR37 and the GR347
merge and follow the same
path to Josselin.*

5Km
1:15

The GR does not go into the village; it crosses
the D122 and proceeds along a former railway
line, then goes up to the right on a farm track,
crosses a road and, by a pretty, sunken path,
reaches the hamlet of Brancillet. Turn right,
then left on to a dirt track which goes up
through the woods and alongside the park of
the Château de Josselin. When you meet the
road, follow it to the left and then immediately
take the dirt track on your right; follow it to the
left to the crossroads to enter Josselin.

JOSSELIN
🏠 🏘 🏕 ✕ 🍷
🚃 🚌

*Josselin is a medieval town
overlooking the valley of
the Oust, and was founded
in 1000 on a rocky spur*

beside the river. Notre-Dame du Roncier was worshipped there, and an important pilgrimage grew up. Begun in the 12th century, the basilica was transformed in the 15th century and finished only recently. In the 15th century the old château became a citadel with nine towers and dungeons; the Ducs de Rohan transformed the interior into a remarkable lacework of stone.

Detour, *12km,*
SAINTE-CROIX
Circular PR walk.

14Km
3:30

Leave the town on the GR37, passing the foot of the château and then following the towpath. At the N24, cross the two bridges to the left and take the second path on the right. Go straight along this path for about 1 kilometre, then turn right in the direction of Bréhalé, then directly right again on a track which soon runs beside the canal. The GR passes near the lock at Le Rouvray, then the lock at Bocneuf; in the wet season, the fields on both sides are flooded. It continues below the contour line which borders the Oust and reaches the hamlet of Camfroux. You will see a 17th century wayside cross on the left. Take the road to the right, turn left after the bridge and climb up to the right to meet the D764 at Le Tertre Camfroux; follow the D764 to the left for 80 metres, then turn right along the second country road in the direction of Beauséjour. Cross the bridge over the canal, then the river by a succession of footbridges before gaining Pomeleuc.

Pomeleuc
The chapel of Saint-Melec is part Romanesque, restored in 1635, with 18th century paintings and statues.

4Km
1

Go round to the left of the chapel and go straight up to the road. Opposite you, 80 metres on, is an ancient posting-house. Go left between the houses and the woods to meet the D117 at Cadoret.

CADORET

1.5Km
0:20

Take the D117 opposite (north) then, where it forks, go left towards the village of Les Forges.

LES FORGES
⌂ ✕ ⵀ ⚓

In the town you will find the château and, just in front of it, the well-preserved ruins of a tall furnace. The forges using the region's minerals and charcoal were established in 1756 by the Duc de Rohan. Cannons were forged there for the royal navy.

6Km
1:30

Leave the town by a minor road to the left (west) in the direction of Bas Bois, cross the Lié by two successive bridges, then proceed straight ahead as far as the Bas Bois farm; there, take the towpath. Cross the footbridge over the narrow canal, and go right to cross another branch of the water. After the lock of the Lié, cross the canal and take the towpath to the right. The GR approaches the village of Griffet; at the crossroads, it continues straight ahead on a gravel path, then goes down to the right and almost at once turns left to meet a minor road; follow this to the left; 80 metres further on, go up a path to the left, then go down to the right again on the minor road to meet, on the left, the crossroads of the bridge of Le Redressement. Take the road to the left, then climb up a footpath to the right which comes out at a country road.

Country road (L'Ecu)
Detour, *20 mins*
ARNÉ
⌂

Go west along the road; there are arrows to mark the way.

The monastery of Timadeuc was founded in 1843 and recognised as an abbey in 1846; it was constructed in the pure Cistercian style, with some materials from the former château of the Rohans.

The GR continues straight ahead; there is a quarry, and the chapel of Saint-Maudan to the left. Descend to the right 1.5 kilometres further on, cross the Oust by two footbridges to meet up with the mill of L'Ille. Go left along the towpath and cross the canal to climb up to the abbey of Timadeuc.

9Km
2:15

The canal from Nantes to Brest

In 1802, Napoleon Bonaparte noticed the exceptional position of Pontivy, in the heart of Brittany and straddling two seas, and decided to designate it the political surveillance centre for the Breton peninsula. Bonaparte had canals dug out, leading from Brest to Nantes and to Lorient, passing through Pontivy. The canal from Nantes to

Take the lane on the left to meet the former marking for the D2, turn left along that and 200 metres further on, cross the new road; follow a track after a bend to the left, take the footpath down through a copse, cross the stream which feeds the Etang de Quengo and climb up to the right to a country road; take that straight ahead and go down again to the left, where you will find a good viewing point. Below that, go to the right. Cross the bridge and follow the towpath to the right to enter Rohan.

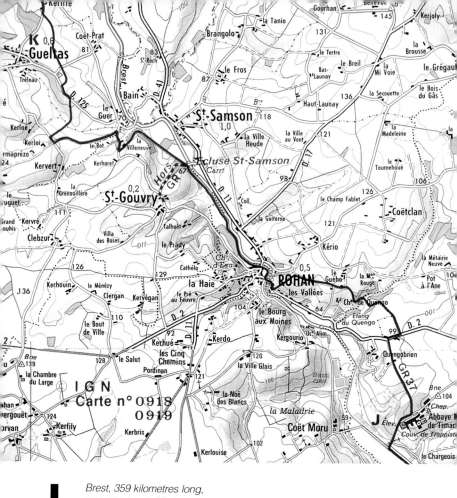

Brest, 359 kilometres long, was constructed between 1806 and 1842. Its traffic was never very heavy and it fell out of use in less than 100 years.

Near the bridge is the chapel of Bonne Encontre. Founded in the 12th century, it was rebuilt in 1510 by Jean II, Vicomte de Rohan.

ROHAN
🏠 ⚓ 🍴 🍷 ⛵

Go along the towpath out of the town to the Saint-Samson lock.

Ecluse de Saint-Samson

Detour, *15 mins,*
SAINT-GOUVRY
⌂

5Km
1:15

Take the road to the left in a south-south-west direction.

Leaving the lock, take the continuation of the towpath, a gravel path which comes out on a road which you take to the right (north). Then take the country road to the left (west) for about 1 kilometre. At the first crossroads, turn right twice and follow a dirt track which crosses a stream and meets the D125.

D125
Detour *15 mins,*
GUELTAS
𐂷 ⚓

Follow the D125 to the left.
The ladder of locks:
Twenty locks have been built over 4.6 kilometres each of a different length, for a difference in level of 60 metres. Each pond has its own charm, flora and fauna.

7.5Km
1:45

At this level, the canal from Nantes to Brest is entirely artificial. It crosses the forest of Branguily and requires 20 locks 3 kilometres apart, to rise over the 48 metre difference in levels.

The GR takes the D125 for about 50 metres and turns right (north) on to a path that passes near the hamlet of Keriffé. The GR crosses the canal and follows the towpath to the left to the lock of La Forêt.

Begun in 1828 and finished in 1838, the Hilvern channel was conceived as the feeder for a string of 24 locks on the Nantes-Brest canal, starting from the Bosmélac dam.

Take a gravel path to the right and continue straight ahead on a footpath which goes across the woods to meet the Hilvern channel. Follow the channel to Saint-Gonnery.

SAINT-GONNERY
⌂ ✕ 𐂷 ⚓

The Château de Carcado, built in the 16th century, is 3 kilometres to the north. Jean Le Sénéchal, Baron de Carcado, was born there. He was killed at the battle of Pavia in 1525, having thrown himself on top of François I in order to save the king's life.

3Km
0:45

Following the Hilvern channel, leave the town; 200 metres further on, take a path to the left, then a road to the right; cross the N168 and proceed along a dirt track, on which there is a lookout. The GR rejoins the Hilvern channel at Ravaguen, crosses a railway line and takes a track which leads to the junction with the GR341.

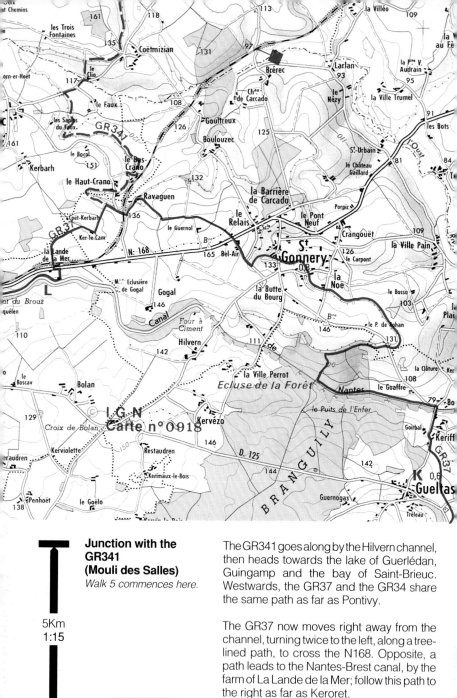

Junction with the GR341 (Mouli des Salles)

Walk 5 commences here.

5Km
1:15

The GR341 goes along by the Hilvern channel, then heads towards the lake of Guerlédan, Guingamp and the bay of Saint-Brieuc. Westwards, the GR37 and the GR34 share the same path as far as Pontivy.

The GR37 now moves right away from the channel, turning twice to the left, along a tree-lined path, to cross the N168. Opposite, a path leads to the Nantes-Brest canal, by the farm of La Lande de la Mer; follow this path to the right as far as Keroret.

KERORET (N168)

Detour, *15 mins,*
SAINT-GÉRAND
✕ ❢ ⊒ ☕

*Romanesque/Gothic
church; old yew-tree;
calvary; war memorial.*

*16th century chapel
restored in the 18th
century; remains of some
stained-glass windows.*

**9Km
2:20**

PONTIVY
⌂ ◠ ⚔ ✕ ❢
⊒ ☕ ▤ ⬒

*Pontivy owes its origins to a
monastery founded in the
7th century by Saint-Ivy, a
monk who came from
Great Britain to convert
Brittany. The town became
the fief of the Rohan family,
who built the château in
1485. To the north is the
medieval town, with its
tangle of streets around the
picturesque Place du
Martray; old church;
château.*

**3.5Km
0:50**

STIVAL
✕ ⊒

*The 16th century Gothic
chapel of Saint-Mériadec
was built on the site of a
hermitage where Saint-
Mériadec lived in the 6th
century.*

**13Km
3:15**

Stay on the north bank to walk along by the nine locks of Bel-Air. The GR proceeds along a minor road which passes near the village of Saint-Drédeno.

Continue straight on; at Kergouët, cross the canal and take a track below it. Go under the railway on the towpath, and go up through the undergrowth on a nice footpath. The GR crosses a road, then runs along by the Saint-Caradec lock and the ponds of Le Roz.

The Saint-Caradec lock is the first of a series that enables you to cross this high ground (`Roz' means·hill).

Follow the towpath, with the chapel of Le Roz on the left, until you reach Pontivy.

The GR37 does not go into the town. Cross the Nantes-Brest canal and walk along by it until you reach the first footbridge on the left; cross this, turn right, cross the water and continue to the right as far as the area of La Plage. Once again cross the water and turn right. Taking a footpath to the right, you meet the N164, which you follow to the right for 100 metres. Take the stony path on the right which leads to Stival.

Proceed straight ahead and, at the end of the village, take a sheltered path opposite which reaches the farms of Kernaud, where there is a viewing point; go through the hamlet and climb up to the left on an old wooded pathway, to Kervéhaut. Continue westwards on a land regroupment track; at the Fournan farm, turn right then left to reach the D15. Follow this to the right; 1,200 metres further on, turn left towards Locmaria, where there is a chapel. Turn right 500 metres on, then left and again right to reach Kermavio. At the end of the hamlet, take a path to the left to reach Coët

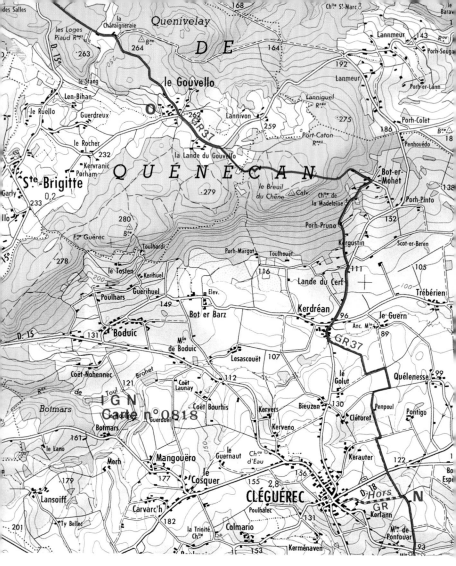

Crossroads
Detour, *15 mins,*
CLÉGUÉREC
🏠 ⛺ 🍴 🍷 ⛴
🚌 📄
Go left at the crossroads.

Moustoir, then the chapel of Saint-Jean. Cross the Guernic stream to the left - you will see a mill - and the D15, proceed straight ahead and pass a house to meet up with the crossroads.

At this crossroads, the GR turns right, crosses the D18 and continues on the land regroupment paths in a north-north-west direction. You will reach the hamlet of Kerdréan, at the foot of the Quénécan massif.

The Quénécan massif, ranging from 250 metres to 280 metres in height, constitutes one of the most beautiful oak and beech forests in Brittany.

**8Km
2:15**

After passing the Forges de Paimpont and the Forges de Lanouée, the footpath will now come to the Forges de Salles, in the forest of Quénécan. Cross a road, then 800 metres further on (see point 111 on the map), take the second road on the left; it passes near the 18th century chapel of Sainte-Madeleine, situated at the edge of the forest; turn up the second path on the left and, at the end of it, proceed along a footpath to the left. At a crossing, climb up the narrow footpath to the right and continue along in the same direction (west).

**Detour,
Le Breuill du Chêne**
Wayside cross and view over the countryside of hills and valleys. Take a footpath to the left off the GR.

Go down the other slope by a footpath through the woods and moors to meet a path which, to the right, leads to a minor road; to the left, this reaches the village of Le Gouvello.

Le Gouvello
'Govel' means a forge.

In the village of Gouvello, go north-west straight along a gravel path through woods to La Châtaigneraie, and then to the Étang des Salles.

Detour, *35 mins*
SAINTE-BRIGITTE
⚔ ⛴
Follow the road to the left.

**4Km
1**

Warning: the GR now crosses a private estate: follow the marked route with great care; do not drop any rubbish; do not smoke; do not pick any plants; do not camp on this land; dogs must be kept on the leash. Continued use of this pathway depends on the walkers respecting the rules. If there is a drought, walking in the forest may be forbidden by prefect's orders.

Detour, *300m to the left,*
The Château des Salles
The ruins of a former château of the Rohans

The GR turns right before reaching the dyke, and arrives at the ruins of the mill of Les Salles.

Moulin des Salles

Junction of the GR37 and the south branch of the GR341, which follows the south bank of the Guerlédan lake (see Walk 5).

Detour, *45 mins,*
LES LOGES BAUCHÉ
⌂
Take the GR341 as far as the Forge Neuve, then take

At the mill cross the dyke and take the little road opposite; 100 metres further on, take the footpath which climbs up to the right. A little before a house, turn right, then right again, arriving at some rocks.

the D15 to the right.

On the right is the Saut du Chevreuil lookout.

The GR follows the forest path to the left (west). Cross the surfaced road and climb up opposite. Arriving on the flat, turn slightly to the right, then 300 metres on to the right again, then left. Turn right on to a little road, then left. Pass a farmhouse, take the little footpath amidst the gorse, keeping to the right. Go as far as the windmill, where there is a lookout. Continue to the right along the footpath. On the tarmac road turn left, and at the crossroads, where there is a wayside cross, take the gravel road on the left, lined with big trees. Turn right at the first house, then 50 metres further on, turn left to a field. Continue straight on through the undergrowth at the edge of the field, and then on a path which descends to the Abbey woods. At the first crossroads turn right. You will come out at the road near the bridge over the canal. Turn left to cross it, and to reach Bon Repos.

6Km
1:30

BON REPOS

Ruins of the abbey of Bon Repos, founded in 1172. It became a cloth factory, a barracks for the Chouans (Royalist insurgents during the Revolution), and quarters for the workers on the Nantes-Brest canal. Rather splendid 18th century buildings surround the site of the former cloister. The remains of the chapel date from the 13th century.

Continue as far as the N164bis, and go left along it. Go on past the D44; 50 metres afterwards, take the minor road on the right, then the pedestrian pathway which rises gently to the crest of the Gorges du Daoulas and towards the place where the GR37 and the GR341 meet.

1Km
0:15

Junction of the GR37 and the GR341

The GR341 arrives from Loudéac by the north bank of the Guerlédan lake; it heads north towards Laniscat, Guingamp and the bay of Saint-Brieuc.

Detour, *45 mins,*
LANISCAT

Go north along the GR341.

From the crossroads, the GR37 follows a westerly direction across the moors, the Landes de Liscuis. You walk beside covered paths at an intersection of old Roman roads.

The research group in Rostrenen considers these megaliths to be evidence of a civilization already

Proceed west across the moors overlooking the site, passing by a ruined farm. Go down by a footpath and meet a broader path, take it to the right and leave it on the right at a bend.

6Km
1:30

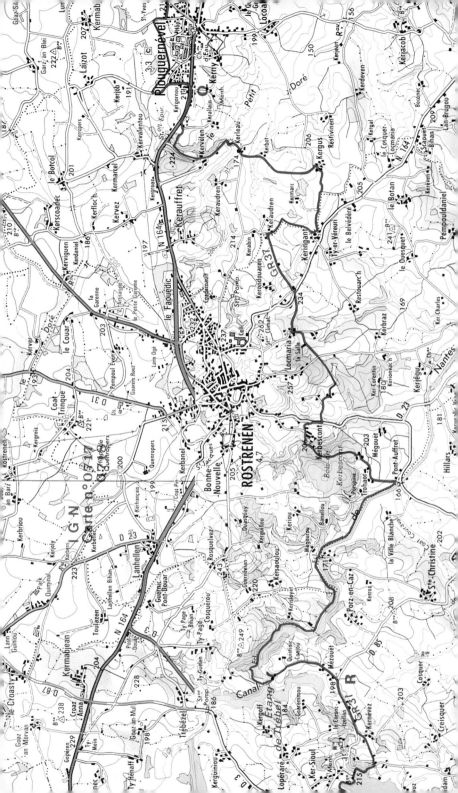

*able to make very
sophisticated use of metal.
The megalithic chain marks
out a network of mines,
situated on the gold-
bearing border of the
granite massif. The stones
in the basin are ancient
mortars for grinding the
gold-bearing rocks; the
present of gold-ore has
been confirmed by
soundings.*

GOUAREC

A 🍷 🚂 🚌

*This town, situated on a
prominent bend of the
Blavet, has old houses,
including the hunting lodge
of the Rohans. The church
was constructed in 1825
on the site of a chapel
dedicated to Notre-Dame
de la Fosse. Gouarec is the
see of the Bishop Audrein,
assassinated by the
Chouans.*

**8Km
2**

PLOUGUERNÉVEL

🍷 🚂 🚌

*The church dates from
1715. You will also notice
the buildings from a former
seminary (1669), now a
hospital.*

**6Km
1:30**

KERMARC

⌂

**3Km
0:45**

Chapel of Locmaria

15th century chapel
Detour, *15 mins,*
ROSTRENEN
🏨 ✗ 🍷 🚂 🚌

*The barons of Rostrenen -
chronicled since 1068 -*

**2Km
0:30**

Further on, the GR goes up across the moors again, crosses a `pass', goes down again to the right and across a little wood. You will meet a broad path; go left at the crossroads and left again on a footpath. Cross the stream to the right at the level of an old mill and go up again to the left to Ty-Baron; follow the road and turn slightly to the left at the next two crossroads. Go down a footpath to the left at a bend in the road, and go up again to the right by a sunken path. Go left to the town of Gouarec.

Leave Gouarec by the D8 and follow a dirt track to the left, the former railway track linking Carhaix and Loudéac. Keep straight ahead and take the second road you come across on the right. Go through the villages of Kerdélès and Quinquis Fulen and go right on the former railway track again which leads to the town of Plouguernével.

The GR leaves the former railway in the north, then comes back to it, thus skirting the town. Take a minor road to the left which meets the N164bis in the south at the hamlet of Kergornou. Follow this road to the right for 300 metres, then descend to the left as far as a most picturesque old stone bridge. Take the road to the left which goes along the valley. At Kerleau, go left as far as Kergus, where you turn right in a westerly direction.

The GR proceeds west towards Keringant. Go right, then go left twice to meet up with the N164. Opposite this, follow the path which leads to the chapel of Locmaria.

figure in all the important historical events of Brittany. There is a 15th century collegiate church and fountain, also the Chapel of Saint-Jacques.

N790
Detour,
Rostrenen
Follow the N790 to the right (north).

The scheme to build the canal was put forward in the 17th century; work was halted by the Revolution, taken up again by Napoleon and finished under Louis-Philipe.

11Km
2:45

GLOMEL
Å ✕ ⟁ ⚓

This trench, 20 metres deep, was dug out in the last century by convicts during the construction of the 2 kilometre long canal.

3Km
0:45

Junction with the GR38
Detour,
SAINT-PÉRAN
⌂
At the junction, take the GR38 for several metres then the fork to the right.

10Km
2:35

At the second road you cross, there is a chapel on either side of the canal: the chapel of Saint-Eloy (right) where, until several years ago, the annual blessing of horses took place; the chapel of Lansalaün (left), with a stained-glass window from 1528.

Go left along the road, then right. At the crossroads, take the path opposite which goes to the farm of Ker Anna. Continue to the N790.

The GR takes the N790 to the right, then takes the first road to the left to reach Kerbescont. Walk southwards along by the wood and you will meet the canal at Pont-Auffret. Follow the towpath to the right. There are wooded areas and numerous offshoots of the canal.

Cross the canal before you reach the Étang de Trébel and climb up the other slope on a winding path. At the exit from the hamlet of Mézouët, take the D85 on the right. At the bend, leave the D85 to follow a minor road opposite, then go down to the right alongside the Étang du Coronc. Cross the dam and walk left along the north bank as far as a campsite. Proceed north-east to reach Glomel.

Go north out of the town. In a wood you will come across the Glomel trench.

Cross the canal and climb up again to the left to take the towpath as far as a bridge (see point 176 on the map) where there is a junction with the GR38.

The GR38, called the `Landes de Lanvaux', enters Redon having crossed the Montagnes Noires, Gourin, Baud and Rochefort-en-Terre.

Proceed westwards along the towpath, then leave it to go right at the hamlet of Kerangall, following a path which leads to the Kerdélen farm. At this point you will encounter the towpath again, and should follow it westwards.

Coming out of the wood on the right, the GR leaves the towpath by a path leading to the village of Leinhon, where there is a viewpoint; follow a little road through a pretty valley in the direction of Le Moustoir.

LE MOUSTOIR

8Km
2

Railway line
Detour, *15 mins,*
CARHAIX-PLOUGUER

*The Romans made it a
busy commercial and
military centre, and built 9
main roads going out of it.
Plouguer church, in the
Romanesque and
Renaissance styles; church
of Saint-Tremeur, with a
tower from 1529 and
Renaissance reredos; 15th
century Sénéchal's house.*

Take the N164 through the town. Opposite the church, go left as far as the hamlet of Sibinel. There, take the road descending south towards the valley. At the Goariva bridge, climb up again to Kerléon, which you bypass. Follow a sunken path northwards to the right. The GR then heads west and crosses a road. Go south, passing close to Kergoutois. Then take the road on the right; turn left and right again to meet up with an old railway line.

You get to Carhaix by the north-west road or by the old north-east railway line.

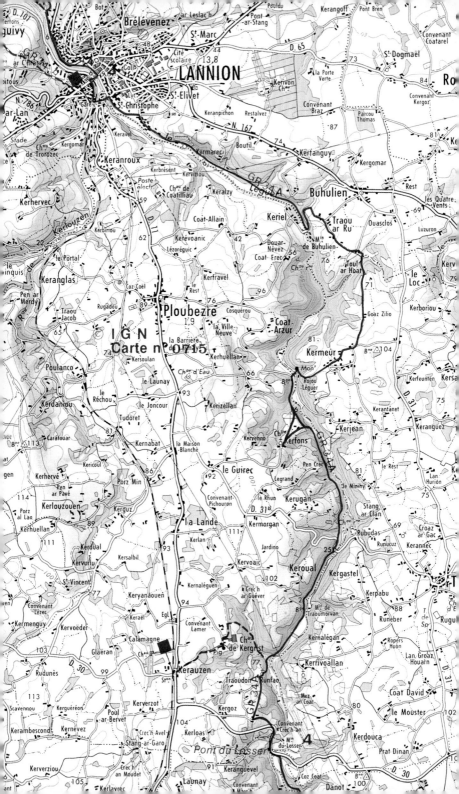

WALK 4

LANNION
🏠 ⌂ ✗ 🚉 🚌 🚐

500 metres to the right ruined mediaeval chateau of Coat-Frec.

At the station the GR34a goes over the level crossing, turns left and then right, and beyond the Kermaria bridge takes the Guingamp road to the right. Turn into the first small road on the right, go past the quarry, and carry on along the path beside the river to a road, near the Buhulien mill.

Take the road to the left, then the first track to the right and the road to Traou ar Ru. At the T-junction turn left, go round a building and take the footpath beside the meadow. After the stream continue into the copse opposite on a small footpath which becomes a small road. At Kermeur turn right and go through the hamlet. Continue along a track, then a footpath down to the river. Cross the bridge, and turn onto the first track on the left. Cross the wood. The track follows the river's edge, and at the edge of the wood climbs up to the right, to the 15th century chapel of Kerfons, with a magnificent roodscreen.

14Km
3:30

By crossing the river it is possible to go up to the mediaeval chateau of Tonquédeec.

Come back to the river, cross two meadows to the right, return to the footpath through the wood, pass the mill, and carry on along the footpath by the river to a tarmac road, the D31B.

The GR34a, keeping to the same bank, takes the footpath opposite through the woods beside the river. There is little waymarking; this is private property.

At the second spillway there is a broad track to the right which leads up to the 15th and 17th century château of Kergrist.

Detour , *30mins*
KERAUZERN
🚌

Detour (see left). The GR34a goes behind a house, climbs up through a copse, crosses the meadow and reaches the chapel of Runfao, or Saint-Fiacre. Taken the tarmac track to the left and the first track on the left, go past a farm, follow the footpath round the field on the left, then the track to the left. Go down the D30 road, left, to Pont du Losser.
   After crossing the bridge the GR34a immediately turns right beside the Léguer,

PONT DU LOSSER
✗

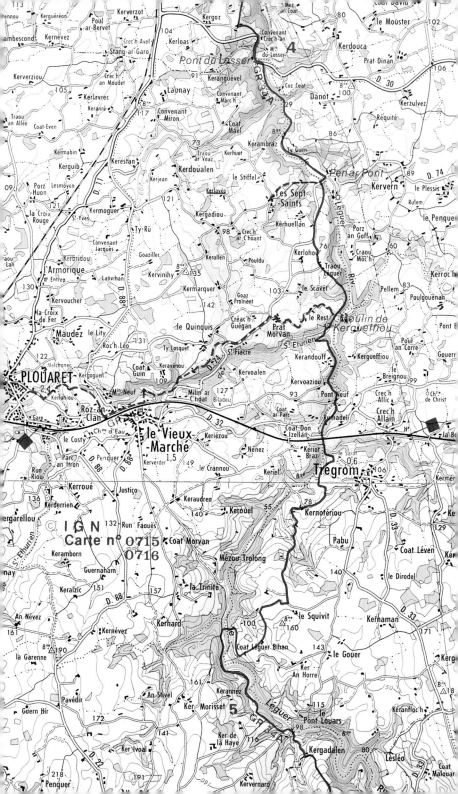

2Km
0:30

Bridge across the Léguer
on the D74 road

2Km
0:30

Detour, *15 mins*
Les Sept-Saints
The chapel of Les Sept-Saints is an extraordinary blend of three religions - pagan, Christian and Islamic. The choir is built on a dolmen, forming a crypt, and there are seven saint's statues enthroned there.

Junction with the GR34

Detour, *15 mins,*
Railway halt at Trégrom
Go back up the D32 to the left, then along the first road to the right.

sometimes on a footpath and sometimes through fields. It comes out on the D74 road: cross the bridge.

The GR34a follows the track to the left after the bridge. Turn left on the road, and take the first dirt track to the left. At Traou-Léguer take the track to the left; at the wood, turn onto a footpath, left, and carry on through the field alongside the hedge. Follow the stream on the left, cross it, and carry on to the Léguer; go upstream to a small bridge close to the Kergueffiou mill, to the junction with the GR34b.

At the bridge, carry on upstream beside the Léguer across marshy open ground to the confluence with the Saint-Eturien, and go upstream beside this river through a field; cross it by a footbridge. Cross the field, and take the track straight ahead, through the wood. At the top of the wood go along the edge of the field on the left. Take the track down to the Léguer, across two meadows, and continue beside the river up stream through woods and then fields. Come out behind a watermill, go round it to the right, and cross the Léguer by a small bridge in front of the mill. Shortly after, turn right, go past a house, and carry on to the tunnel under the railway.

The GR34a goes through the tunnel. Continue a short way to the left, cross over the tributary of the Léguer by a wooden bridge on the right (if it is in flood, go back up the stream to cross it more easily). Go up the track opposite, and turn right just before the farm. Cross a small stream, go up the broad track to the left, and turn right.

At the cross, Kernotériou, turn left on the road which then becomes a track. Go past Groas Deillo, take the track to the right just past the transformer, towards Coat Léguer; turn onto the footpath to the left. On a level with the high tension line, cross two fields, and at the house turn right and then left beside the ruin. Take the small road to the right, and on a

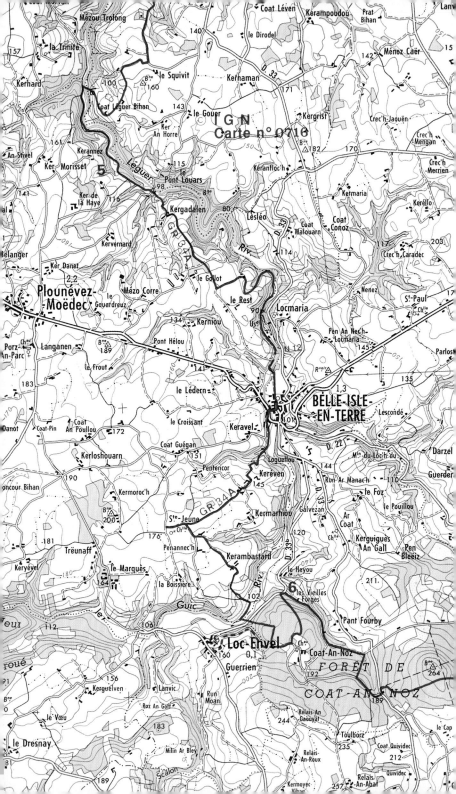

bend turn off it to the right, into the wood to the river; cross the river by the wooden bridge. Turn left and follow a track upstream by the Léguer, sometimes moving slightly away from it. Cross a track and carry on in the same direction.

14Km
3:30

If the track is impassable, go up to the right then turn left and left again along footpaths, to join up with a broader track; turn right along this track.

Cross the road near a bridge, the Pont Louars.

Take the small road which extends to Kergadalen, then the track to the left which becomes a road.

Turn left to Kergouedic; at the farm, take the dirt track to the stream, and walk beside it to the left, through the wood, to the Léguer.

Go upstream beside the river, and cross over the first wooden bridge; carry on upstream between the two branches of the Léguer: there may be slight modifications to the path. Come out by a house, go round it, and take the road under the viaduct. The GR crosses a bridge on the left, goes along by the sports ground, and on to the church square in Belle-Isle-en-Terre.

Belle-Isle-en-Terre

2km to the north, the 14th and 16th century chapel of Locmaria, with a magnificent roodscreen.

Beyond the church the GR goes past the front of the *mairie*, turns right on the D712 and then takes the road to the left. Carry on to a mill, then take the track which continues on from it; come out onto a small road, turn right, and take the small dirt track which is almost opposite, by the end of the house. Follow the lane which it leads into, to the Sainte-Jeune chapel.

Come back onto the same road, and carry on along it, turning off down the road to the left and then off again to the right. At Kerambastard, turn right between the houses and take the first track on the right, then on the way down turn left. Cross the river by a small bridge, cross the road, go up the track through the woods opposite. On the flat open ground turn right, to come out onto a forest road.

Detour, *20 mins*
5Km
1:15
Loc Envel
Pretty 16th century church.

1Km
0:15
Chateau de Coat-an-Noz

LES VIEILLES FORGES
⚠ ♵

10Km
2:30

Gurunhuel
✗ ♵ ⚒

Detour *(see left)* Turn right along the road. At the edge of the wood take a small footpath to the left, go round the back of the cemetery, to the church of Loc-Envel.

The GR continues to the left on a road on the Château de Coat-an-Noz.

In front of the chateau take a footpath through the woods to the left (north) and carry on to the D33B. Turn right onto it and shortly afterwards take the track to the right to Les Vieilles Forges.

After about 1.5 kilometres, leave the track on a footpath to the right. Turn left onto a road through the wood.

Come out onto the D33 by a forest house at La Barrière Blanche. Turn left, and immediately take the forest path on the right; after 150 metres turn right onto a small footpath, and then after 100 metres carry on along the widest footpath on the left.

Cross a very wide forest path and carry on almost straight across, at the edge of a plantation of young conifers; the track is difficult to see here. Then take the small footpath to the right, then take the broader track on the left. Cross the Léguer by a wooden footbridge to the right.

If the footbridge has been swept away by flood, go downstream by the river to the point at map reference 132. Cross the bridge and go back upstream by the track on the other side.

Beyond the footbridge the GR continues straight on to a wide forest path. Turn right, then shortly after take another path up to the left. When it first levels out, take a straight path to the right, east. At the T-junction, turn left, and cross a small stream. Take the first track on the left, turn right and then left. Turn onto a footpath to the right, then turn left, then right, onto the forest road. Beyond a barrier go straight on, and shortly after take a track to the left; go past Le Faut, and turn left into a track. Cross the D54 and take the track opposite and then the D54 to Gurunhuel.

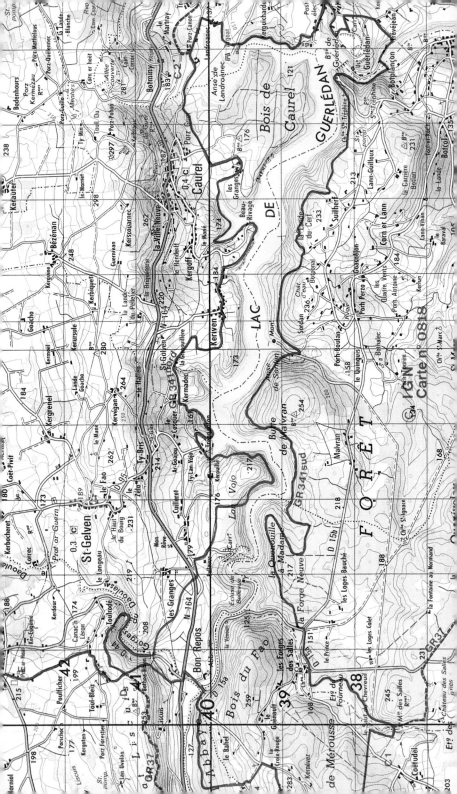

WALK 5

This route begins at the GR37 near Saint-Gonnéry (See p. 40). It leads round the Lac de Guerlédan in an anti-clockwise direction, as far as Gurunhuel.

Moulin des Salles
(Junction of the GR37 and GR341)
(See map ref.C1)

From Moulin des Salles the GR341 south heads eastwards along the south bank of the lake, then up its western bank to the Porz Canon crossing. We are unfortunately not able to provided more detail.

Porz-Canon crossing
(See map ref. C2)

At the Porz-Canon crossing turn right. Take the broad dirt track on the left as far as the second crossroads.

Detour, *15 mins,*
CAUREL
🏠 ⌂ 🍷 ⛴ 🚌

4Km
1:0

At the crossroads of the dirt track and the road, take the latter to the right as far as the village. In the near future this may be altered to enable hikers to get near the lake, so follow the markings carefully. Follow the road which is a continuation of the dirt track. Take the Route des Granges on the left. Having passed the farm, take the path across fields to the edge to the lake, which you walk along on its left. You will come to a little road; continue along by the lake. Pass between the restaurant and the lake to come out at the parking area. If the level of the water allows you, continue along the little roads (to the right and twice to the left) as far as Beau-Rivage.

BEAU-RIVAGE
⛺ 🍴

4Km
1:0

Take the road along the lake; turn left. At Kériven, continue straight ahead on a path. At the house, turn twice to the right, then twice to the left. The path meanders along the edge of the field. At a sharp-angled crossing, go left in the direction of La Grenouillère, then continue straight ahead. Shortly after Kermadec, turn left to enter a wood and go down to the lake. Climb up again to the right to an old slate-quarry. On the crest, go left down towards the lake, which you walk beside until you reach Trégnanton.

TRÉGNANTON
⛺ 🍴
(Warning: loose stones underfoot)

Follow the little surfaced road on the right. After a bend, take the surfaced path on the left, which almost immediately becomes a footpath. Go over the ridge and descend into

a valley on the other side. Cross the stream opposite and continue straight ahead beneath the pine trees. Approaching the lake, turn to the right. Walk along the edge of a meadow for 50 metres and turn left. Skirt the rocky ridge, which you walk alongside on the right. Before the summit, go down towards the lake again, along by a rock face, then follow the lakeside on the right.

Pass two rocky spurs and, after an embankment, climb a very steep slope to the right. Keep to the ditch and do not go into the meadow. (NB: be careful not to break the wire as you leave, as the maintenance of the route depends on it.) Take the path which continues from the ditch and curves to the left. You will come out on a little surfaced road; turn right, then to the left. Turn right at the back of a former level crossing keeper's house. Cross the N164 road and take the old railway line, which is raised a little at the start. Before going over the viaduct, go down to the left into a valley and climb up the valley of the Daoulas gorges by the D44 road on the right. At a bend, take the footpath which climbs to the summit, then go left along the ridges (the path is difficult because it is overgrown with gorse). After two ruins, cross two meadows and take the footpath which comes out on the crest of the Daoulas gorges and at a GR junction.

8Km
2:15

Meeting point of the GR37 and the GR341(north)
(See map ref. D)

3Km
0:45

The GR341 goes right. At the corner of a house, turn right, then left and right on a surfaced road, which you follow until you reach a transformer. Turn left then right on to the D76, which takes you into the village of Laniscat.

LANISCAT
⌂ △ 𝗫 ✕ 𝖸

Church built in 1691; bas relief; wheel with chimes.

In front of the church, turn left along the D95 in the direction of Sainte-Tréphine; 200 metres further on, take the little surfaced road to the left; 400 metres after the village of Goazillou, go left on a track footpath which becomes gravel path to the D95. Turn left, pass a chapel and over the stream, the Sulon. Go left in the direction of Fontaine-Gouarec, then the road becomes a farm track.

Turn left on to the surfaced road, then quickly to the right in the direction of Kerfolben. At

Kerfolben, go along the farm track to a cross. Continue straight ahead. At the first crossroads, go right to reach Le Cosquer. Turn left at the wayside cross. Continue along the dirt track opposite. Take a path to the left, which curves right, and then left again. Pass Kernaonet, go down to the left. Go along by the hedge which borders the field on the right. (The entry is a bit difficult to spot.) Take the little road continuing on, then turn left and, at the hamlet of Pen-ar-Lan, take the surfaced road to the right. Pass Garzolès. Continue straight on, cross the new D790 and proceed to the ex-D790, which you take to the right as far as the swimming-pool, (The lines for the Saint-Nicolas detour have disrupted the GR. This will be improved in due course; follow the markings carefully).

16Km
4:0

SWIMMING-POOL
Y

(Pisc. on the map)

Detour, *20 mins,*
SAINT-NICHOLAS-DU-PÉLEM
🏠 ⚐ ✗ �#️ 🚌

15th century church; nearby, 17th century Saint-Nicolas fountain; in the area, chapels, manors and standing-stones.

Follow the D790 to the right, or the minor roads either to the left or the right of the main road.

Turn left. Head towards the valley of the Faoudel, taking a little surfaced road as far as the mill, then a gravel road. After crossing the stream, take the path on the left which leads to an old farm, and after the farm climb up the footpath on the left. You will come out on a dirt track, which you take to the left to the village of Kergoubleau. Take the tarmac path, almost opposite a gravel path. Turn right towards Kerlévenez. Pass to the left of the manor, take the path running on from it beside the undergrowth, and then along the course of the Blavet. At a stone bridge, continue along by the Blavet, go upstream of a little tributary, which you ford just before crossing the D8. Rejoin the course of the Blavet after having walked alongside two sections of land. As you come out of the wood on to a meadow, you will see the junction with the GR341a.

11Km
2:45

Junction with the GR341a

Turn right along the GR341a.

Detour, *1hr,*
LANRIVAIN
✗ ♀ ♨

5Km
1:15

TRÉMARGAT
♀

Church of Notre-Dame;
wayside cross; a standing
stone.

Detour, *500m,*
TY NEVEZ
⌂

13Km
3:15

The GR341 itself crosses the Blavet on granite blocks. (If the Blavet is in spate, cross a bit further back on the large rocks of the chaos, or make a detour via the fields as far as the next little road.) Go down river on the right bank. Keep to the undergrowth, never use the bridle paths; meeting a footpath, you cross the riding track and take a lane opposite which goes along by the Saint-Georges stream. At a ford, leave the lane to walk along a footpath even closer to the steam. (NB: permission to use this path is conditional on the quietness and unobtrusiveness of hikers.) Remaining on the left bank of the Saint-Georges stream, continue upstream. You emerge on a dirt track at the level of a little dam; cross the field on the dyke and take the footpath opposite, then the dirt track to the right. After the school, turn right to reach the village of Trémargat.

Take the D87 towards Kergrist-Moëlou. At Quinquis-Auffret, turn right and soon afterwards right again on to a dirt track. When the path is not usable, walk in the field which it borders. You will come out at Le Hellè on a surfaced road, which you take to the left as far as Guernavalou.

Turn right towards Toul-Holton. Take the footpath to the right, which is damp and overgrown, between the plantations of firs and larches. You will come out at a dirt track; take this as far as Le Goaffr. A little before the farm, go left, cross the Saint-Georges stream and continue along the footpath opposite, or in the neighbouring fields if the path is unusable. (Do not use the right-hand path after the stream.) Go through Kerfaven and continue on the tarmac path to the D50A, which you take to the left in the direction of Loc'h. Go past the Kerbidiry crossroads and take the gravel road after it, on the right. Cross the stream from the Étang du Loc'h, and go on to Kerléon. Turn left twice in a row, and continue for 200 metres along the road. Take the gravel road on the right to Kermorvan, where there is a megalithic tomb and a stele. Turn right, then left at the next house; the footpath is difficult to see at the beginning. Go on to Kerohou, the druids, centre. Proceed to the D50, and turn left, as far as Maël-Pestivien.

MAËL-PESTIVIEN
✗ ♈ ⬥

Church, with stained-glass windows, pietà and rood-loft.

Before the church, take the D28 to the right and turn left on a gravel road soon after the D50 (the Bulat-Pestivien road). Cross the footbridge over a stream. Continue across the moor, where the path is damp and not easily discernible, and follow the path to the manor of Kérauffret.

KÉRAUFFRET
⌂

Coming out of the manor, go left and soon right on a dirt track. Pass a hedge. Take a road to the left, which is tarmac and then gravel, to Kerbalen. Continue straight on through the village, then take a path to the right which leads to a lookout over the Etang du Blavet. Retrace your steps, crossing the village of Kerbalen and the D20. Take the dirt track opposite, then the first one on the right. Cross the tarmac road and proceed opposite to cross a stream - this is a very damp area. Turn slightly left, first alongside a field, then on a broad path. Turn left at a farm. Take a path which climbs up from the road, then join the country road for 150 metres. At the wayside cross, take the footpath on the right. Turn left at the mill, to come out on a tarmac farm track to Kernaléguen. Follow this path to the right as far as Kermac'h. Turn right then at once left on to a dirt path which runs into the D50 to Bulat-Pestivien.

12Km
3:0

BULAT-PESTIVIEN
⚠ ✗ ♈ ⬥

15th-16th century church.

Retrace your steps by road and path in the direction of Kermac'h. Take the dirt track on the left, which runs on across a field. Take the footpath which turns left, then turn right. Cross a tiny stone bridge. Take the dirt track on the right to Porz ar Goff, and continue to the right to the 16th century chapel and cross of Pestivien. Take the tarmac farm track opposite the chapel to Kerluff. Take the very damp path which runs on from it, and climb up the bank on the left. Walk along the top until the bank ends; turn left after the stream. Cross the D24A and the village of Coz Caroës. Take a dirt track to the right between the houses and at the edge of a small pinewood, turn left near a farm on to a tarmac road.

6Km
1:30

Detour, *30 mins,*
PONT-MELVEZ
♈ ⬥

Take the minor road to the right, then to the left.

Turn left. Soon after the Darlac'h farm, take the gravel path to the right. Continue straight ahead on the farm track. You will come out at a little surfaced road, the D31, which you take to the right to reach the D787.

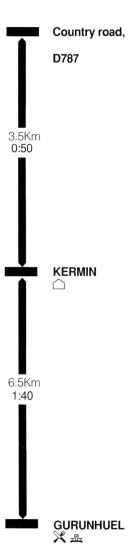

Country road,

D787

3.5Km
0:50

KERMIN

6.5Km
1:40

GURUNHUEL

Church; wayside cross with figures. This is the junction with the GR34a coming from Lannion.

Proceed along the little road opposite. Cross the railway line. Take the first gravel path on the right, which leads to Grouannec. In the village, cross a tarmac road and immediately take a path on the left. Turn on to a little dirt track on the left. Go right, on to a minor road and at the first crossing turn right to reach Kérambuan. Where five roads meet, take the first on the left towards Kermin. About 50 metres on, go left and follow a path - often used by cattle - then, on a footpath through the undergrowth, which more or less follows the river, to another path. Take this to the right to quickly reach a road onto which you turn left. Continue to Kermin.

In the village take the road to the right, then to the left. Continue along the tarmac road. At the crossroads of four roads, follow that on the left, which gives a fine view tof the whole region. At another such crossroads, take the path on the left as far as the tarmac road, which you take to the right, to the pretty, restored chapel of Saint-Fiacre. Go past the chapel and take the path on the left soon after the first farm. If the path is too muddy, go through the fields and pastures. Turn right along the tarmac road, and before Lan Verc'h take a path to the right, which turns left and passes the Roudannou farm. Cross the road, take the path opposite to the left, and after the stream, turn right. Pass the hamlet of Guern Hir, turn right then left towards Le Miniou. Turn right to reach Gurunhuel.

WALK 6

This walk begins on the GR34 Tro-Breiz to Saint-Brieuc (Port du Légué) in the neighbourhood known as `Pont Tournant' (swing bridge). Leave Le Pont Tournant and head right until you come to the roundabout on your left, making you way along the quay to the first street on your right. Turn right along a path which meanders along behind the water purification centre and crosses the valley of Gouédic. When you leave the valley, cross La Rue de Gouédic and take the steps opposite the entrance to the car park which lead to the Rue W.-Rousseau, almost in the centre of Saint-Brieuc.

SAINT-BRIEUC

🏛 ⌂ ⚓ ✗ ☖
🚉 🚌 🚐 🛈

Cathedral; old town

10Km
2:30

To follow the GR371 southern route, continue along the street on the right and go down some steps again on the right. At the bottom, turn left under the bridge. Leaving the footbridge behind, descend again into the Gouédic valley. As you emerge from the valley, turn right along the Rue de Trégueux, and then left at the roundabout along a lane which passes behind the campsite. Cross a road and come to a car park, where you should continue to make you way round the Étang de Robien. When you have passed a culvert on your right, turn right again along the Rue F. Villon, which will bring you out on to the former N778 (Saint-Brieuc to Vannes) road. Follow this left for 200 metres. Turn right along the narrow Rue des Villes Cadorées, then left, and then cross over the railway bridge. When you reach the roundabout take the Rue de la Victoire; then take the Rue des Noës which becomes a cul-de-sac; at the end is a sunken lane. You will come to a road, just after a building lot, where you should turn right and then subsequently left along a gravel path which, after a while, follows the railway line. Keep the level crossing on your right and follow the road for 400 metres. When you pass a house, take the grassy path on your right which winds its way to a farm; cross the access road leading to the farm; and then take the path opposite which borders the railway line on the left. When you come to the bridge, follow a path which makes its way along a narrow valley through the trees until it reaches a lane.

Here is the junction with the northern part of the GR371 which leads back to Saint-Brieuc.

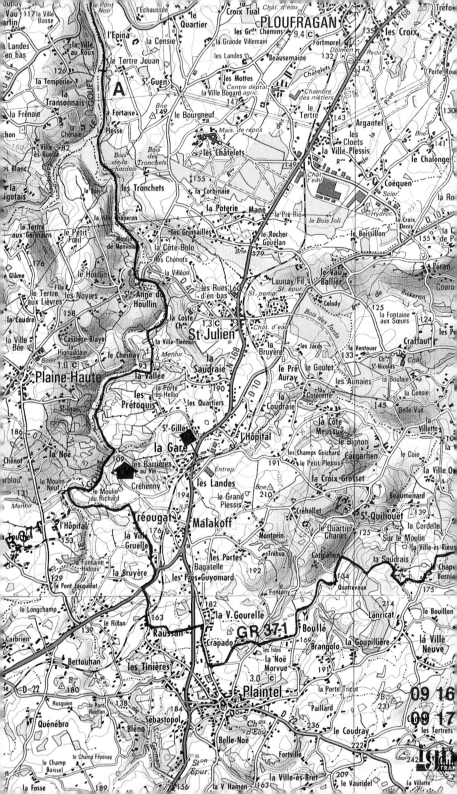

The road on your left will bring you into Pont-Noir.

Pont-Noir

6.5Km
1:30

Go under the bridge and then walk along the right bank of the Gouet reservoir on a path which meanders through the woods. (You can also follow an unmarked path along the left bank. There may actually be more viewing points on this route, but it will take longer.) Turn right along the road to Sainte-Anne-du-Houlin.

SAINTE-ANNE-DU-HOULIN
🏠 ⌂ 🍷 ⚓

There is a good view from the top of the rise from, where you can see a standing stone in a field, the Château de la Coste in the distance, and a manor house above Sainte-Anne-du-Houlin.

6Km
1:30

As you enter the village, turn left along a track which follows the right bank of the River Gouet. The track narrows to a path through the trees. Head diagonally across a meadow on your left, and join up with a path which climbs up along the edge of a wood. A track on your left will bring you to a road. When you come to some houses, turn twice right along recently surfaced lanes until you come to a footbridge with a ladder at water level; take the fisherman's path on your left which follows the course of the Gouet: follow it closely. Cross the Gouet rapids, and continue along the fisherman's track, leaving it for a moment to pass behind a house.

MOULIN DE RICHARD `MALAKOF'

Follow the river through woods and across meadows. When you have passed the houses on the other bank, you will come to a crossroads where the GR routes intersect. Make sure you don't turn along the route which heads right across the river towards Quintin.

Junction of the two branches of the GR371

5Km
1:15

Stay on the same side to the river and continue straight on along a track which climbs up to the left above the river. After the first crossroads continue on the right, then head right again after the clump of fir trees. The tack becomes a tarmac lane and subsequently turns into a dirt track. You will come out on the D790, where you should turn right and then left 200 metres later along the small tarmac road. Shortly after the level crossing, take the dirt track on the left. Cross the D778 (which has 4 lanes) and take the track opposite. This will bring you out at a tarmac road, where you should turn right.

Detour, *10 mins*
PLAINTEL

16Km
4:0

Turn right towards Saint-Quihouet, and then left 50 metres later towards Crapado. Cross a road and take the lane opposite to Boullé. At the first crossroads, turn to the left along a small lane. Go through Boullé, and shortly after a deserted farm take the dirt track on your right. Turn right again at the edge of the wood and then left when you reach the top. You will come out at the village of La Saudrais, where you should turn right and then left along the small lane immediately after the last house in the village. Cross two fields and then turn immediately left along a small road which quickly becomes nothing more than a dirt track. Take the first lane on your right and continue along the small tarmac road. Cross another tarmac road and take the path opposite. This takes you along beside a thicket. When you come to a bend in the road, go down the meadow on the left, running alongside the embankment as you do so, and then cross the stream. The path opposite will take you up to the right to the village of L'Isle.

Turn along the lane on the left which looks down on the stream. Turn left into the meadow, past a small bridge, and then continue straight on, turning right shortly afterwards. When you come to the tarmac road which leads to Le Rochay, turn right and then immediately left along a lane. Continue straight on to the D27, and make your way across to the small gravel lane opposite. Turn right along the small tarmac road, and then left 150 metres later along a lane which narrows to a path. When you come to another tarmac road, turn right. Continue straight on along the lane until you reach the crossroads. After 150 metres turn right, cross a small tarmac road and continue along the small road opposite. Continue straight on along the path until you come to another crossroads, then head right. Turn right along a small tarmac road, and then left immediately after the village of Couëssurel. Turn left 50 metres after a water pumping station, go past a stream on the right and take a rather vaguely marked path into a copse. Turn right along a gravel farm road and head through the village of La Braize. Cross a tarmac road and take the passage opposite, which is shaded by large

trees. Then turn right along the first paved lane you come to, and right again along the tarmac road.

Detour, *20 mins*
SAINT-CARREUC
🏥 ⌂ 🕴 ✕ 🍷
🚊

Continue straight on for 800 metres. The Château du Plessis is 880 metres outside the town.

Stay on this road towards the small town for 50 metres and then turn off left along a path. You may find that you have to make your way along the edge of the field at this point. Turn left at the edge of the wood, and continue on round the trees, actually venturing into the wood where necessary. When you come to the end, head right. You will come out at a tarmac road, where you should turn right. After 50 metres turn left towards Le Vau Gouro and then left again 50 metres later. This will bring you out on a small tarmac road, where you should turn left again. Turn right when you come to the D81, and right again along a metalled road towards La Teurtrée. Make your way through the village and take the first tarmac road on the left. Pass through Le Val and Cariza. Shortly afterwards, head right towards Le Fébillet; just before the farm turn left along the lane which heads into the undergrowth and meanders cross-country. Turn left when you come to a dirt track. You will now find yourself on a small tarmac road; turn left, cross over the D25 shortly afterwards, and take the dirt track opposite which heads into the fir trees. Turn right in the wood: a sunken lane will take you out into the open again. Continue along the small road and turn left when you get to the transformer at Pellan along a small tarmac road.

9Km
2:15

Detour, *30 mins*
HÉNON
⌂ ✕ 🍷 🚊 🚌
Continue straight on for 2 kilometres.

5.5Km
1:30

Turn right towards La Ville Norme. Before the house, take the dirt track on the left. After the stream continue on the right. Go past a ruined building. When you reach the hamlet of Les Alleux, take the lane on the left and then turn right at the edge of the wood. When you leave the trees behind, take the right branch which leads to Chêne Loyo farm. Turn left, 300 metres later turn right along a lane which follows the old railway line. Follow this lane to the station at Moncontour. Cross the N168 and take the road to Launay mill. When you come to the stadium some 500 metres later, turn off the tarmac road and head straight along the lane which passes to the left of an old people's home. Continue along the Rue des Hautes-Folies; when you

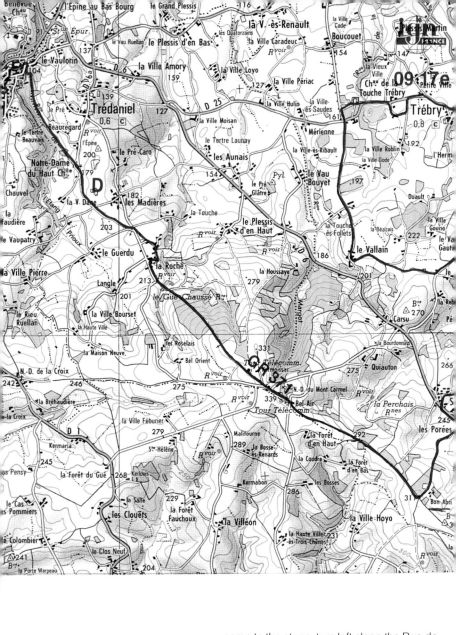

come to the steps, turn left along the Rue de la Pompe and then left again along Rue Notre-Dame. Head right along Rue de la Victoire, which brings you out at La Place de Penthièvre.

MONCONTOUR

🏠 🅰 ✕ 🍷 ⚒

🚌 🚃

This is an old fortified town and is worth a visit. 16th century Saint-Mathurin church, with its 6 magnificent, 17th century stained-glass windows, and marble high altar (1768); 16th, 17th and 18th century houses.

2Km
0.30

Notre-Dame du Haut

14th/16th century chapel; fantastic statues of Notre Dame and the saints with healing powers; the fountain.

The chapel here has a good panoramic view. Note the curious outline of the trees on this hill, which is the topmost point of the Côtes-du-Nord (339 metres). There are 8 lines and a circle, representing the sun, which was worshipped here. (See map ref. D)

21Km
5:15

Detour, *on the right.*
The Saint-Maudez chapel

Built from the remains of an old chapel. There is also a dolmen.

Go down the Rue du Temple opposite. Turn right behind the church along the Rue du Docteur-Sagory and then left along the Rue du Champ-de-l'Avoir. Shortly after this, climb up the Poterne Saint-Jean and L'Eperon steps, and take the Rue Saint-Michel opposite. Turn left along the Rue de l'Aire-Domois 100 metres later. At the end of the street is a small path slightly to the right; follow this as it meanders along for about 1 kilometre. Cross the stream and climb up among the rocks. When you get to the top of the small slope, turn right along a small path which leads to Notre-Dame du Haut.

Follow the tarmac road opposite for about 2 kilometres. Pass through the hamlet of La Roche and 200 metres later, when you come to a bend in the road, take the small road straight ahead and then the second lane on the right. Climb up into the woods along this lane, which becomes metalled at the edge of the trees and stretches to the crossroads just after the TV transmitter.

Leave the TV transmitter on your left, and follow the path along past the farm for about 2 kilometres. (The boundary follows an old Roman road.) Turn left, go past the Bon Abri farm, and rejoin the D6. Follow this left to the village of Saint-Mieux. As you leave the village, take the lane on the right alongside the hill. When you come to a farm, turn left to the Vaux farm; when you get there, turn left along the small road towards the village of Le Vau Gauthier.

Just before you get to the village, turn left at the fork and make your way up to Le Carouge. Follow the track towards the dolmen. Turn right just after this monument, and shortly afterwards, just before La Ville Gourio, you will see signs to the Étang de la Ville Gourio, which lies 500 metres off the GR.

Turn left and follow the small road to Le Vallain; then turn right along the small road which leads to the Château de la Touche Trébry, which is open to the public in the summer. Go past the château and you will come out onto the D25, which you should follow left around the lake. Take the first small

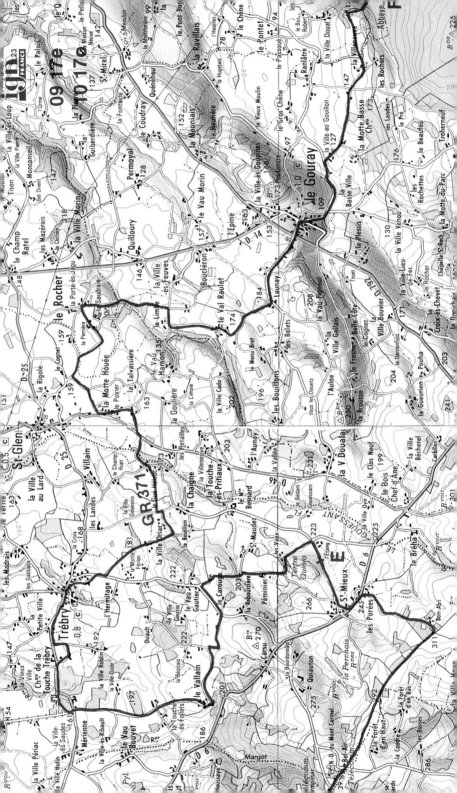

road on you right and cross the hamlet. When you come to the crossroads, turn left to get to the D25; then turn left along this road to the market town of Trébry.

TRÉBRY
✕ ♀ ⚓

Taxis can be ordered from Mme. Annie Dutertre.

11.5Km
3:0

Turn right after the church along a lane which heads between two houses, and follow this to a road where you should turn right for 50 metres. Turn left along a track, make your way through a hamlet and then take a small road on the left to La Ville Oriac. Shortly afterwards, you will come to another road, where you should turn left. Then turn right along the first lane which leads to Le Gué Héleuc; when you reach the hamlet, turn right and then immediately left along a lane which will bring you out on the D46. Follow this to the left and you will soon come to a sunken lane on you right. Now turn left along the small road which leads to La Motte Houée. After the village turn right and then bend gently left . At the next crossroads, turn first right and then left. You will pass an avenue leading up to the Château de la Saudraie, which is now a holiday centre belonging to Saint-Brieuc. Make your way through a hamlet, turn right alongside a fence, pass the stream and then climb up to a crossroads. Turn right towards Le Limbe and then head left towards Le Val Raulet. When you get there, take the road which leads to Le Gouray. Avoid the two lanes on your left, continue on past the sports ground and the cemetery, and then descend towards the market town of Le Gouray.

LE GOURAY
⌂ ✕ ⚓

Make your way past the church and turn left towards Boquen Abbey. Turn left again along a tarmac road. Pass a farm with a water mill, and then turn right along the road to La Ville-neuve. Continue along the lane, cross a field, and then follow the lane on the right again before turning left along the lane leading to Boquen Abbey.

Boquen Abbey
Founded in 1137, and was then rebuilt and restored from 1936 onwards; it has a 12th century nave and transept, a 14th century flat chevet, and a 12th century capitular room. Look out for

When you get to the abbey, take the road on the left followed by the one on the right, and make your way up the incline. Turn right along the lane which leads down to Guillaudière, and then right again along the road to La Bèrnais. Go through the village, turn right, and then head up towards the covered walk at La Brousse. You will join up

the stone in the middle of the path as you approach the church: it bears the imprint of a donkey's hoof.

24Km
6:0

Detour, *550m*
Dolo
Turn left off the GR.

JUGON
⌂ Å ✕ ⛾ 🚉

with the D59 on the left; follow it, keeping the D39A and then a small overgrown track on your right. Shortly after this, turn right along the small track which plunges into the overgrowth and leads to a small road where you again turn right. As you turn left, you will pass the road leading to the Château de la Moussaye, which you will seen in front of you. Take the good lane immediately on the left, although this subsequently deteriorates to a sunken track. As you leave the wood, turn right along the lane which leads to a crossroads. Here you should turn right and then immediately left and left again along a lane leading to La Touche Joubin. At the crossroads, follow the road opposite which goes through Saint-André, then La Ville Liard and on to Le Bilieu. Turn left along the road to La Clos Batard and past the farm. At the junction, turn right underneath the four roads and then turn right again over the railway bridge to La Touche-ès-Gautier. When you get to the tiny village, turn left and so down the lane to the road, where you turn left again. When you have passed the cemetery, take the lane leading to the tarmac road.

Take the road opposite to Le Bouquet Jalu. Turn right along a lane and follow it until you come to a lake. You can now make your way round the lake to Jugon, so long as the level of the water permits. If not, turn left at the viewpoint and join up with the road again, which will take you right to Jugon.

You will come to the dam across the lake. Descend to La Place du Martray, cross the square and then cut across the D106. Continue on towards the church, and follow the River Arguenon. When you come to the concrete column supporting the viaduct, take the footbridge across the Arguenon and follow the good path along the right bank: this climbs up to the left and joins a small road, where you should turn right. Continue on through the hamlet of Les Loges and shortly afterwards, when you come to a bend in the road, turn right along a track which will take you into the wood. Follow a path through the wooded dell which descends towards the Arguenon. Follow the bank for 100 metres, turn first left along a good track and then right

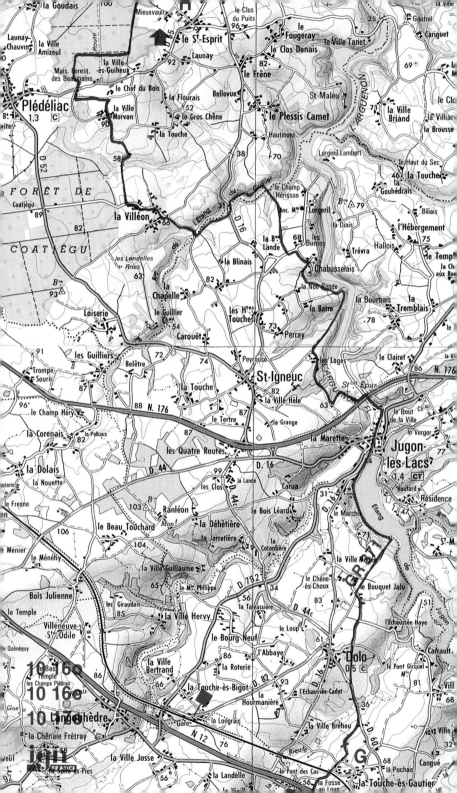

18Km
4:30

D55

Detour, *15 mins*
PLÉDÉLIAC
✗ ⚒

Interior of the 15th century church.

Detour, *15 mins*
LE SAINT-ESPRIT
⌂ Å ✗ ⵏ ⚒

CHÂTEAU DE LA HUNAUDAYE
Å

Here you can see the imposing ruins of a 13th and 15th century feudal château.

along a path which runs around the edge of the wood. Make your way round La Planchette pond and you will come to the tiny village. Now take the small road on the right and turn left when you reach the cross. Turn left again 200 metres later, and then shortly afterwards take the track on the right which goes down to the stream feeding the Étang du Guillier. Cross over the footbridge, and then follow the stream left until you come to the D61; now turn left underneath the bridge. A path on the right 80 metres later will plunge you into the wood and will lead you along the right bank of the stream to a small road at Pont Balène. Cross the bridge and turn right along this road. When you come to another road, turn left. When you reach the village of La Villéon, turn right and then further on, after the outlying houses, turn right along a small road and cross a little bridge. Continue to the right, then turn left at the crossroads. You will come to La Ville Morvan, where you should turn right. At the next crossroads turn left along the small road, and then take the next road on the right which will lead you straight to the D55. Cross over this to the forest.

Shortly after entering the wood, follow a track on the left to a forest path, and then take this to the right. Turn right again at the next track you come to, and then take the second track on the left, which veers right.

When you get to the crossroads; take the road almost opposite; turn left at the next junction and then take the good path on your right followed by a wide track, also on the right. Cross over the D61, and continue on the small road opposite. When the road bends, continue straight on along a track which narrows to a path and leads to the Château de la Hunaudaye.

Take the path running round the left side of the ruins, which brings you out on the D28A. Turn off this immediately by continuing straight on towards Saint-Jean. Before you actually get to there take the good track which climbs up to the right. Pick up a small road, and turn first left and then right to La Denais. Veer left through the little village, and when you have passed the last house, follow the track which

descends to the right and narrows to a path. Cross over a small stream, and you will come to a picnic area and then a small road, where you should turn left. Cross over Tournemine bridge. Shortly after this, as you begin to climb, take the small road which makes a hairpin turn left and brings you out at Cariguet. Continue until you come to a road, where you should turn left. You can seen a small lake to the right of the road. When you come to a crossroads, which marks the site of an old school, turn left along the D60 and then, shortly afterwards, left again and then right.

Go through the hamlet of Le Frostel and continue almost straight on before turning right back towards the D60: follow this left for 400 metres. Wade through the stream on the right and continue along the track to Les Pruniers farm. Now follow the good track on your right, and then turn to the hamlet of La Treunais. Continue straight on past a pond on your right. Shortly after this, turn right along the small road, cross over the D792 at Champs Ménard, and head towards Saint-Méloir. After 50 metres, turn off on the small road leading to La Ville-ès-Rieux and, at the next crossroads, take the good track leading to the chapel of Saint-Méen. As you approach the first houses, turn right and then left. You will come out beside the church in the square, where you should turn left.

You are now on the D92, but should turn off this at the end of the square and continue straight on along a small road which narrows to a track and then a path, taking you towards Lardillais. You will come to a good track and 300 metres later, after a field, you should turn left along a large tree-lined path. Skirt round the left side of La Ville Rue manor house, cross over a farmyard, and you will fine that the road veers right. Take the small lane immediately on your left opposite the entrance to a farm, which runs along the edge of a field and then turns to join the first houses on the D89.

14Km
3:30

D89

Detour, *200m*
SAINT-MÉLOIR-DES-BOIS
⌂ ⵣ ⵣ

Turn left along the D89 and then head right after the outlying houses along a narrow road towards La Ville-es-Brets; turn off this to the right when you come to the first houses, continuing almost straight on along a track which will take you to the D91. Cross over the

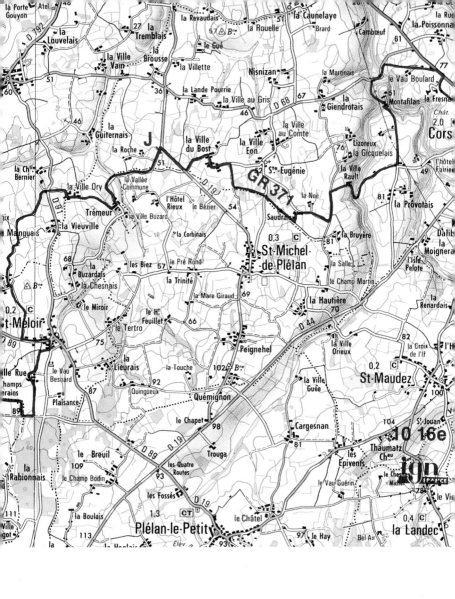

Boundary stone; Le Miroir manor house.

road and take the lane opposite. When you get to Trémeur, turn left and then immediately left again. A small bridge will take you over the spillway of the lake; continue on, taking the small road on the left which will bring you out on the D19. Turn left here towards La Ville du Bost and make your way through the village. After the last farm, turn right along a small road and take the track on the left 150 metres later.

Detour, *1km,*
SAINT-MICHEL-DE-PLÉLAN
⌂ ♈

12Km
3:0

There is a fine monolithic cross at the crossroads.

CORSEUL
⌂ ⌂ ⚴ ✗ ♈
~~

This old capital of the Celtic coriosolite clan had its heyday in the Gallo-Roman era, but fell into decline in the 4th century.

When you enter the market town, you can see a fine monolithic cross 80 metres down the first street on the right. Close to the entrance to the church is a caryatid holy water basin, and in the south transept, in the corner of the south wall, there is a Roman funeral stele, which has been translated by Mérimée. The town hall houses an interesting Gallo-Roman museum. There are remains of columns around

Cross over a small road and continue opposite. At the crossroads turn left towards Le Saudrais. Turn right and turn off to the right at the first crossroads. Then turn left along a small tarmac road, and then right along the land leading to La Ville Rault. Continue on, cross over the river, and climb up straight ahead past a ruined windmill. You will come out on a small road, where you should turn left.

Further on, a small path on the right will take you to the ruins of the Château de Montafilan.

Shortly after this, follow the small path on the left, which descends towards Montafilan stream, crosses over the bridge, and takes you along the left bank to the D68, where you should turn right. As you begin to climb, a good track on the right will lead you to the D794.

Shortly after this, turn along the small road on the right which narrows to a lane and veers left. You will pick up the D794, which brings you back into Corseul.

Turn right before the church, take the second street on the left, and then turn right along the D794 towards Dinan. Shortly before you come to the last houses, turn right along the track which runs between two stone pillars. At the end of the path turn left, and after the farm make your way round the fields to a small road, where you should turn left. Just before you come to the D794, follow the lane which climbs up to the right - this is an old Roman road - and then when you come to the crossroads, take the small road on the right. You are now close to Haut Bécherel farm, which houses an octagonal `cella', a room which used to be a holy place or `fanum' dedicated to Mars.

Turn left at the next crossroads, make your way past the hedge in front of the farm, and then take the track on your left which leads to the D794. Turn left along this road for 50 metres, being sure to take care as there is a lot of traffic but rather poor visibility. You should then turn right along a small road towards La Ville Quematz, and right again

the building, and a tomb of a Roman woman in the church.

16.5Km
4:10

Detour, *600m,*
QUÉVERT

Continue to the right.

VALLÉE DE LA FONTAINE DES EAUX

An old spa specialising in thermal cures.

Intersection with the GR34c

1Km
0.15

This heads left along the Rance to Dinard.

DINAN

200 metres later along a lane which becomes a sunken track as it descends towards a stream; cross this, and then climb back up to Le Vauhesry. Continue along a small road which narrows to a dirt track and takes you to La Marette. Make your way through the village, and shortly afterwards you will join up with the road, where you should turn right. Cross over the railway line. Turn right along the path immediately after this, and follow it for 200 metres before turning left. Cross over a road, and take the track opposite, which is an old Roman road. Cross over another road and you will then come to the D26. Turn right and then immediately left along a track and then follow the track almost opposite to La Ville Pierre. Cross over the D26, and then follow a sunken lane which meanders around the fields to La Landelle. Skirt the left-hand side of the lake and then climb up beside the stream to the D68.

Turn left along the D68 and go under the dual carriageway. When you come to the Poulichet crossroads, cross over the D2 and follow the footpath opposite to the cemetery, continue along a small street to the D766. Turn right underneath the railway bridge and then immediately left, near to the small chapel: you will find that you are running alongside the railway line at this point. When you get to the end, turn right along the street which brings you out at the school gates. Turn left, and when you come to the small terrace, follow the small path which goes down through the trees into the valley. You should now take the small road on your right, but be careful as this is narrow and rather dangerous.

As you continue along this road, you come to the River Rance.

Make your way right along the Rance to Le Vieux Pont: the Jerzual is on the right.

Cross the bridge, and then turn immediately right. Follow the right bank of the Rance to the

161

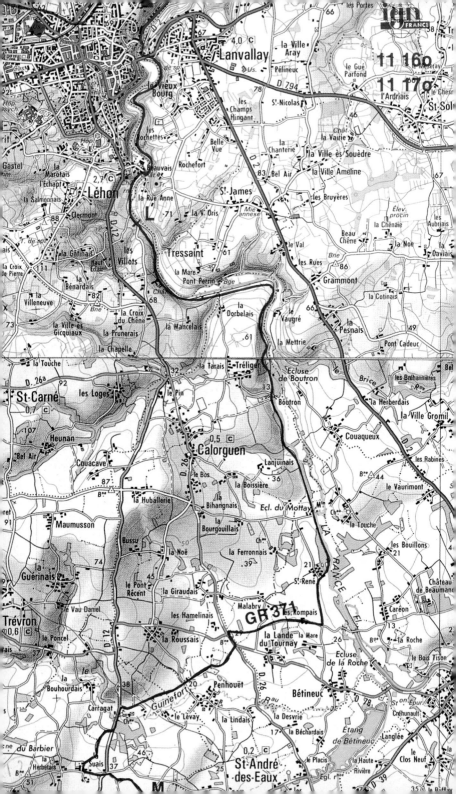

Picturesque streets and battlements dating from the 15th and 16th centuries, 14th century ramparts, castle keep and castle; Saint-Sauveur basilica dating from the 12th, 15th and 16th centuries; the Couvent des Cordeliers; the English garden with its splendid views.

9Km
2:0

Léhon bridge, and then cross over the river again.

Léhon

Old houses; 12th century church; ruins of 17th century cloisters 14th century monks' refectory; ruins of a feudal château.

First make your way south along the canal towpath, and then head east before turning south again. You will pass Boutron lock, and then come to Mottay lock.

Mottay lock

Detour, *2kms,*
EVRAN
🏠 ✕ 🚋 🚃

Continue along the towpath.

Turn off the towpath 600 metres after the lock and the nearby mill, along a track on the right.

After the tiny hamlet of Saint-René, take the road on the left and then turn right towards Les Rompais.

Detour, *1km*
Bétineuc dam
Further on, on the left, you can make a trip round the dam.

The road turns into a rather muddy track, and boots are certainly recommended in the winter. Continue in a westerly direction, and then take a short cut along a road on the left. Head right when you come to a fork - the signs aren't very clear here - and make your way across a private orchard, making sure to keep to the edge. A surfaced track takes you close to an earthen embankment, the old railway line. Then take a hairpin bend left. You are not far from the Château de Carragat.

7Km
2:0

Château de Carragat

Built in 1763 it has cornices with moulded modillions and girded doors with coats of arms. The building looks on to an avenue of trees leading to a chapel.

Detour, *2.5kms*
TREVRON
⌂

Head right along the D12 and then left along the D78.

Continue straight on, and then turn along the D12. Turn right and then almost immediately left along a lane leading to the village of La Suais, where there are impressive farm buildings. Turn left again until you come to the D12.

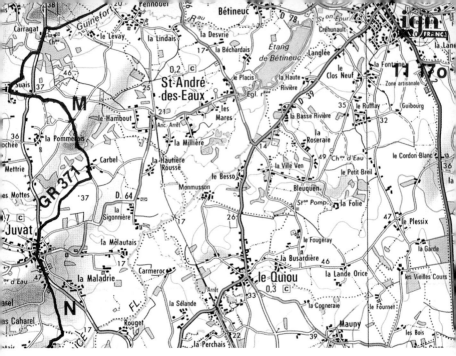

Detour, *3km*
SAINT-ANDRÉ-DES-EAUX
⌂ ⚑

*Take the small footpath
opposite. 12th century
church; many footpaths.*

SAINT-JUVAT
⚐ ⚒

*17th century houses; the
church (1364), with its 12th
century portal: notice the
covered porch, the two
lateral benches, and the
statues on the surrounding
dry stone walls brought
from local calvaries; some
interesting crosses in the
14th century cemetery.*

3Km
1:0

D39
Detour, *15 mins,*
TRÉFUMEL
⌂ ✕ ⚐ ⚒
Go left along the D39 for 1

Cross over the D12 and continue almost
opposite along a dirt track which bends
slightly to the right and is bordered by gorse;
turn left further on, and climb up a track to a
private wood. Cross over the field to the
cluster of houses at Carbel, and follow the
lane on the left which heads south-west. Turn
left when you come to the D12 towards Saint-
Juvat.

Head south out of the market town towards
Tréfumal; when the road narrows, continue
along the lane. Go through a damp area and
then pass a bridge with an iron ramp over the
old Rance before making your way round the
old Rosaire mill: don't try to go inside. Cross
a field dotted with poplars, and then carefully
skirt round the edge of a field which takes you
straight to a track beside the Rance. Cross
the small bridge over the river to the D39.

The GR turns right along the D39 for 300
metres and then left along a lane bordered by
gorse and oak trees. Climb over the fence on

Tréfumel village has been prosperous since the 18th century, because it has traditionally cultivated flax for sails. The refurbished

the right and then another one into a field; when you get to the other side, turn right along a tarmac road. Head left when you reach the first farm, make your way round the edge of a field (which isn't very clearly marked) and cross a small wood. Continue southwards along a pebbly track. Cross over a tarmac

church dates from the 10th and 11th centuries, as does the nearby yew tree.

road and continue opposite to another road. Turn left along this for a while and then turn left into the village of Traveneuc. Go through the village, and then head right. Turn left along a dirt track and left again to the village of Callouet, where you join up with the GR37.

3Km
1:0

GR37
Detour,
RÉNÉAL,
SAINT-PERN,
CARADEUC AND
BÉCHEREL

Take the GR37 to the left.

Flowing through a granite trench, the Rance was dammed up in 1937 so that a hydraulic power station could be built. It is a remarkable location: the banks are sharp, rocky and wooded, and look down on a reservoir which is more than 8 kilometres long, and up to 40 metres deep beside the dam.

First follow the small track on your right which leads to Rophemel reservoir. Continue along the left side of the reservoir until you come to a road, where you should turn right past the Néal bridge.

From the bridge, climb up on the D25; when you get to the hairpin bend which is a feature of the valley, head left along a small track which takes you to Le Feuil. Now make two right turns to Le Bas crossroads, and then take the road left in a westerly direction for 1 kilometre, which will lead to the megaliths at Champ de Lampouy (the Megaliths of Chênot).

6Km
1:30

Megaliths of Chênot
The main monuments, all made from quartz, are on the eastern side and include 8 high standing stones a second parallel grouping disappears into an embankment which runs alongside the west of the field. An isolated 5 metre high menhir stands south of Chênot farm, and another one stands by itself on the other side of the road in the middle of a field.

The route separates from the GR37, which heads south at Chênot farm towards Médréac.

Continue straight on. The lane narrows to a track before becoming a small road again at Les Tréhérols. You will come out on the D89, where you should turn right, and then take the small tarmac road on the left just before you come to Guitté.

GUITTÉ

Saint-Mathurin chapel; the privately owned Beaumont château, which can be seen from the road.

Cross the D25 and continue along the lane which becomes a track after Le Corgnais, where you turn left to cross a stream. When you come to a tarmac road, turn right and after 300 metres take the track off to the left. Turn right along the D25. After the village of Le Mont, take the dirt track on the left and then enter the meadow 100 metres later. Shortly before the Beau Soleil farm, turn right into Couellan wood. Follow the wide path through the trees, heading left as you go. Turn left

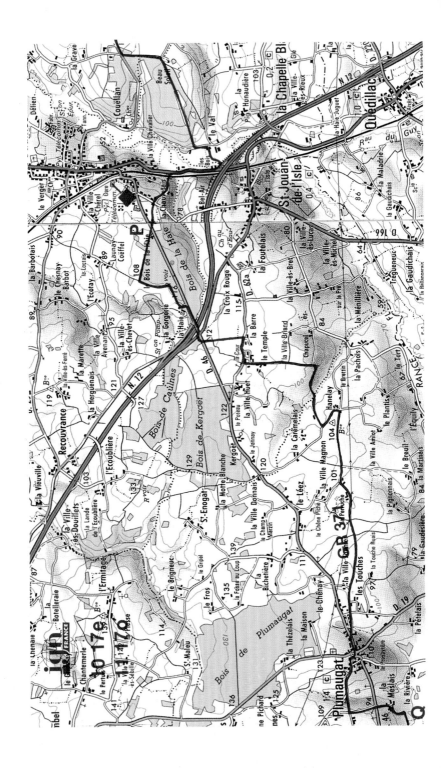

when you leave the forest. When you come to the middle of the village of Le Val, take the track on the right which leads to the Rance. Follow the river for 10 metres or so, and then cross the footbridge.

SAINT-JOUAN-DE-L'ISLE
⌂ ✕

Skirt the restaurant courtyard on your left and you will come to the D766, where you should turn right.

Detour, *15 mins*
CAULNES
⌂ ✕ ♆ ⚓ 🚂

9Km
2:15

Go along the D766 for 15 minutes.
15th century church; Couéllan château; La Hunaudière manor house at La Chapelle-Blanche.

Detour, *15 mins,*
SAINT-JOUAN-DE-L'ISLE
✕ ♆ ⚓

Take the first road on the left which passes under the railway line and then narrows to a track, which turns left before a house. Cross over the D46.

Go left along the D766. Sculptures at the church; the covered markets; Kergouet manor house; the old Château de Saint-Jean.

D46
Detour, *15 mins*
Caulnes
Turn right.

Take the track opposite, which runs through a wood and then alongside it round the edge of a field. When you reach the crossroads, turn left along the lane which runs round the wood. Turn left when you come to the end of the wood, then right along the D46, which runs along above the N12 dual carriageway. Shortly after the N12, turn left along a track and then right along a small road. When you get to Le Temple, turn left and then take the dirt track on the right. After passing a small lake this track veers right. It becomes very muddy and you may have to follow the field which runs alongside to get to a ruined farm. Continue along this track and turn left. When you get to Hanelay, turn right along the track which goes straight to the D46, where you should turn left to Plumaugat.

9Km
2:15

PLUMAUGAT
⌂ ⚑ ⚓
Rectory (1678); Bonne-

Go round the church and continue along the small road. Take the road on the left, and then turn left again. When you get to La Meslais,

169

*Rencontre chapel (1583);
Saint-Yves-de-Bénin
chapel (1609); Bénin
cross.*

take the track on the right. It is usually flooded at the lowest point, and you will have to go through the meadow on the right. You will come out on the D46, where you should turn left and then left again 50 metres later. At L'Epinay, where you can visit the manor-house chapel and dovecote, turn right along the small tarmac road and then left along the gravel track. Then turn right along the track leading to the Château de Loziers. Continue along the wooded walk opposite the château, and then turn along the small road on the right. Immediately after passing the second farm, turn right along the edge of the fields. Make your way round the left side of the lake, the Étang de Loziers pond, and then turn along the track on the right. When you get to Pouha farm, continue along the small road. At the bend after a crossroads, continue along a track. Turn right along a small gravel road which narrows to a track and continues straight on to Les Treize Chênes. Turn right along the D76 towards Saint-Launeuc, and 100 metres later take the track on the left. Veer left again until you come to a tarmac road, the D52, where you should turn right to reach the old railway line.

11Km
2:45

Detour, *300m*
TRÉMORE
✗ 🚉
Les Treize Chênes chapel.

Follow the old railway track right to the D793.

10Km
2:30

MERDRIGNAC
🏠 ⌂ 🛐 ✗ 🚉 🚌
*The 14th century Saint-
Launeuc church is 5
kilometres away. You can
also visit La Hardouinais
forest and lake.*

Continue opposite along the railway line, go past the old railway station and straight on past the holiday village. Cross over the D6.

Detour,
Sainte-Brigitte chapel
On your left.

Cross over two tarmac roads, and 500 metres after the second turn left at a bend. Immediately after this, take a small tarmac road on your left, and then turn right 200 metres later along a dirt track. It may be necessary to leave the track at one point and walk through the field on the left if the going becomes too difficult because it is overgrown. Cross over the N164 - but be careful, as this is a very dangerous road. Continue along the small road to Le Chêne Creux, and then

12.5Km
3

171

continue along the track opposite until you come to a tarmac road, where you should turn left.

Detour, *2kms,*
Saint-Guénaël

Continue along the road on the right to the chapel and ruins of an old windmill.

Cross over a tarmac road and continue straight on. In the middle of the village of Castenouët, turn right and continue along the small road to La Fériolaie. Go through the village, turn right, and then continue along the tarmac road to La Guénaie. Then head right towards Les Vaux Brûlés.

Detour, *250m,*
The standing stone at
La Pellionaie

Continue on to Les Aulnais, where you can visit the château, woods and private lake. Then take the tarmac road left to Gomené.

GOMENÉ
⌂ ☗ ⚒

The church here is Gothic.

Start opposite the town hall, and take the tarmac road for 200 metres. Before you reach the old wash-house, take the path on the left to La Ville Haye. When you get to the end of the village, take the public footpath to La Ville-ès-Pies. Then take the small road that runs between the two farms, and when you come out on a tarmac road, turn left and then take the first tarmac road on the right before the village of Le Vau Dinel.

Detour, *1km*
Continue towards La Ville Menst where you will come to a dolmen.

Make your way along the road for 500 metres, and then turn right along the path which climbs up the hillock to La Ville Louais. From the top, there is a panoramic view over Coëtlogon, La Trinité-Porthouët and Ménéac. Continue along the road and then turn left behind the row of houses. You may find the hedge that grows 100 metres behind the village interesting, as it has a circumference of 5.1 metres. Follow the gravel track, and you will come out on a small road, which you should follow for 100 metres.

Detour, *1.5km*
Roquetton

Follow this road to the village, where there is a chapel and fountain.

Take the small road on the left down to the village of La Chotinière. (After Cargahu, you will see a leafy hillock on your right, which is well known for its legends and its three crosses. You can look out over Laurenan, Plémet and Coëtlogon.) When you get to La Chotinière, continue left to Le Breil Malard.

14Km
3:30

There are some superb granite houses, some frescos and a chapel with a wooden altar 200 metres on your left.

Continue on the D106, where you should turn right towards Cargouët. Turn right again just before the bridge, and follow the road up to the village of Lèquidy. As you leave the

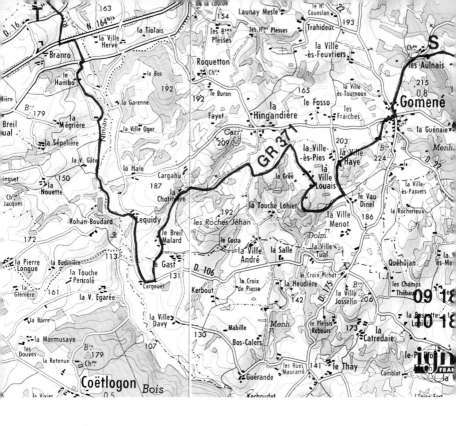

village, take the path on the left for about 20 metres and then go down the path to the right through woods to a mound: watch out, as the first part of this path is rather hidden. The mound is the site of an old water mill. When you come to a small river, walk along the right bank for about 800 metres until you come to the Pont de la Pie. This part of the route is often overgrown.

Cross over the bridge and follow the other bank, gradually working your way away from the river. Go round the foot of the hill, and then cross the small wood. You will come out on a dirt track, which you should follow to Tremoyas. Turn right back towards the river and then follow it left along a fisherman's path. You should turn left along a dirt track which takes you to a tarmac road, and then turn right. Head through Le Hambo, and take the tarmac road on the left. Shortly after this, veer slightly right along a dirt track which leads to the N164, where you should turn left. Take care,

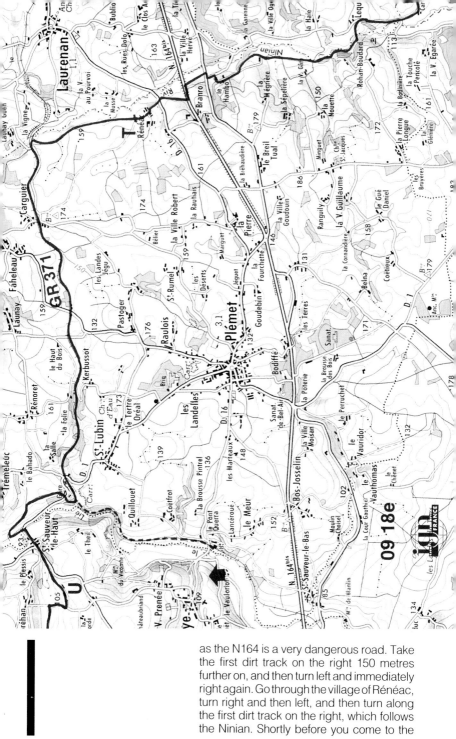

as the N164 is a very dangerous road. Take the first dirt track on the right 150 metres further on, and then turn left and immediately right again. Go through the village of Rénéac, turn right and then left, and then turn along the first dirt track on the right, which follows the Ninian. Shortly before you come to the

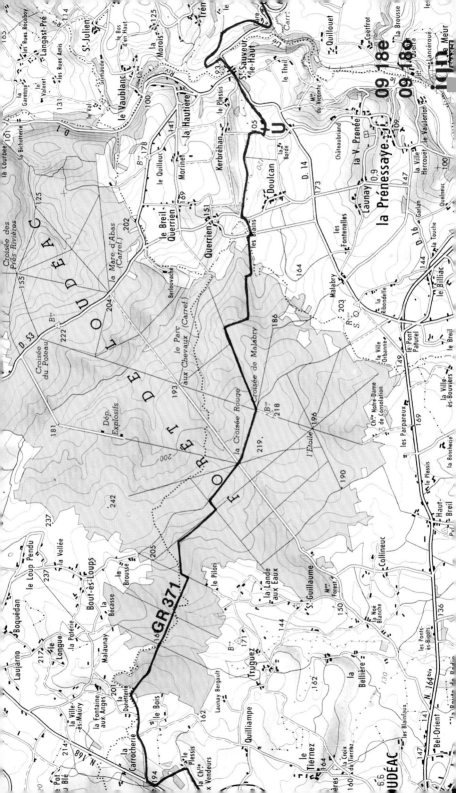

stream, take the track on the left which plunges into the undergrowth and comes out at a railway track.

Étang Launay Guen

Detour, *2km*
LAURENAN
🏠 ◇ ✕ ♈ ⚖
🚃 🚂

5.5Km
1:15

Head right along the railway track.

Follow the old railway track left. go through the hamlet of Carguier - the Château de Launay Guen and its private estate are about 600 metres to the right. Continue straight on, and after crossing over 3 tarmac roads, you will come to Saint-Lubin station.

SAINT-LUBIN STATION
🚂

Detour, *30 mins,*
LE PONT QUERRA
◇

Detour see left.

Continue straight on after the station, past the quarry and follow the old railway line through the magnificent Hêlury gorge. Take the road towards Plémet and the the first road on the right.

Detour , *3km*
LA PRENESSAYE
◇ 🏕 ✕ ♈ ⚖

Detour, *5.5km*
PLÉMET
🏠 🏕 ✕ ⚖

Detour, *600m*
Saint-Lubin
Listed village, chapel.

Just before you enter the station, take the track up to the right. You will come out on the tarmac road, the D1, where you should turn right and then immediately left along a track. This track veers left and then immediately afterwards right when it gets to the top, and then descends into the valley. Turn left when you reach the small gravel road. You will come to a tarmac road which takes you into Saint-Sauveur-Le-Haut, 200 metres further on.

Detour, *2km*
Le Vaublanc
The village is to the right, with its chapel and château.

18Km
4:30

Turn right, go past the bridge and then turn immediately left along a small road. Keep to the left as you walk through the valley. The road narrows to a dirt track. When you have passed through La Ville-Roger, you will come out on a small tarmac road, where you should turn right. Then take the first small road on the left. When you come to the T-junction, turn left and then right 50 metres later. Turn right when you come to the tarmac road, and then immediately take the first track on the left. As you enter the wood, follow a path which veers

slightly right and climbs gently. Continue straight over the first crossroads (marked ONF73) and turn right when you come to a Y-junction. Then turn left along the wide forest track. When you come to the roundabout at La Croisée de Malabry, take the wide path almost opposite, which runs horizontally.

When you reach La Croisée Rouge, follow the track almost opposite (2nd to the left of the cross) and 50 metres after the crossroads you will come to a T-junction. Turn left here, and then right 150 metres later. Half-way down the slope, turn along the third track on the left. When you come to another T-junction, turn left along the wide forest track and then right 150 metres later (ONF13). Continue straight on to the edge of the forest. Then follow the dirt track, between the fields, which will widen to a small tarmac road and bring you to the D768, where you should turn left. Turn left again 50 metres later along a small track which leads to Le Plessis. Turn right along the gravel road, and you will eventually come to the D768. Turn left here, past the level crossing until you come to the D700. Cross the road, and take the small tarmac road opposite. When you come to the TV transmitter, turn left. At the village of Limpiguet, turn right and then left. Cross over a tarmac road, and continue along the track opposite. This will bring you out on a small tarmac road, which you should follow left to the D41.

D41
Detour, *30 mins,*
LOUDÉAC
⌂ Å ✕ ▥ ⛟

▭

Turn left along the D41 for 2 kilometres. Parish church with 8 chapels; the church tower built between 1735 and 1741; the High Altar dates from between 1763 and 1778; 15th century Clos Reland cross.

6Km
1:40

Turn right and then left 150 metres later towards the chapel of Saint-Gilles-du-Ménec. When you reach the chapel continue straight on and follow the first wide track on your left. This track joins up with the GR341b coming from Loudéac, and the two run together to Saint-Guen. Turn right when you come to a T-junction and then left along a small tarmac road. Head immediately left to the Château de la Ville aux Veneurs. After Dugouët farm, turn right along the small tarmac road. This continues straight on, and is the Saint-Caradec to Trévé road. When you come out on the D7, turn left to Saint-Caradec.

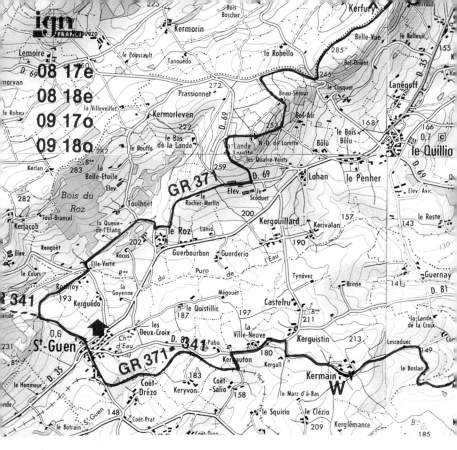

SAINT-CARADEC

🏠 ⌂ 🛠 ⚓ 🚃

There is an interesting parish church, with a crypt and baptistry, as well as the chapels of Saint-Jorel and Saint-Laurent.

15Km
3:45

On the right is the 15th century chapel of Saint Pabu or Saint Tugdual, which has a 16th century wooden rood-screen.

Start at La Place de l'Église and take the D7A towards Saint-Thélo; 150 metres later take the road on the left and follow it to the tiny hamlet of La Croix. Turn right here, and follow the Hilvern channel, along whichever bank is easier. You will pass through Kerléau, Kerdudaval, Le Bâtiment and Kerguéhuic, and will come out on a tarmac lane.

You can see the Commanée manor farm house 200 metres to your right. The path between this point and Saint-Guen may be changed from time to time, so watch out for signs.

Turn left and go through Kermain, continuing straight on when you come to the cross. When you come to another cross with its top missing, turn right to reach the D81, and then turn left towards Saint-Guen. After another 750 metres, when you find yourself opposite

Kergauton farm, turn left along a road, then turn right 250 metres later and follow the old railway track.

Continue straight on along the old railway line. When you come to a tarmac road, turn right towards Saint-Guen.

SAINT-GUEN
⌂ Å ✕ ⅄ ⚓ ▭

Church (1610); fountain; Saint-Elouarn chapel.

Go past the church, cross over the D35 and near the bakery continue, along a small tarmac road opposite. (Watch out for signs, as this is where you separate from the GR341, which carries straight on towards Guerlédan lake, Saint-Nicolas-du-Pélem, Guingamp and Paimpol.) Turn right along a small tarmac road, take the first road on the left, and then turn immediately right along a track. Then take the first road on the right, past the chapel, and shortly afterwards make two left turns. Continue straight on for 200 metres along a tarmac farm road which takes you to the D69. Follow the road straight on for 200 metres. Then take the first dirt track on the left, and then the wider dirt road on the left to the fountain of Notre-Dame-de-Lorette. Now turn almost immediately right along the small road leading to the Notre-Dame-de-Lorette chapel. There is a cromlech here (a circle of upright prehistoric stones). Continue straight on behind the chapel until you come out of the trees. Then turn left along a small road, past Beau Séjour farm and turn along the small gravel road on the right 300 metres later. When you come to the crossroads, turn right along the tarmac road to Le Quillio.

Detour, *20 mins,*
LE QUILLIO
⌂ ✕ ⅄ ⚓

Gasquer château; 16th century church; Saint-Maurice chapel; Marouet cross.

Turn right along the Quillio road, and then immediately left along a tarmac lane for 50 metres, which narrows to a dirt track. Continue straight on until you come to a tarmac road.

Alternative route to Hilvern channel. This makes its way along country lanes and basically follows the hilltops, making it perhaps more interesting than the Hilvern channel. When you come to the tarmac road, turn left, pass Crainfaut farm and take the tarmac road to the right. Skirt a large meadow on the left, and then follow the small path up to the left and at the end of the field continue along a track over the left side of the crest. Turn left along a small road, and then right along another

21.5Km
5:30

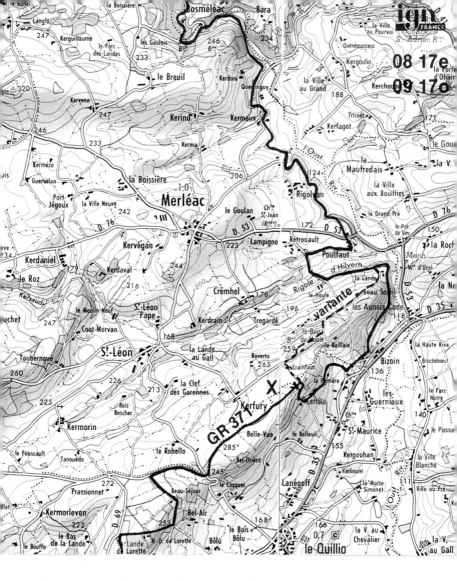

road which descends to the Hilvern channel, where you turn left again.

Turn right and then immediately left after the outlying houses. When you come to a large shop selling drinks turn right and then left along a series of small roads to the Hilvern channel, where you should turn left (it is on your right-hand side when you first come to it). Cross to the left at the first bridge (against the flow of the current). Cross over a tarmac road and then turn right along the next tarmac road you come to. Continue to make your way along the right of the Hilvern channel (left bank as regards the actual flow of the current) until you come to the outlying houses. Turn left and cross over the D53 at Poulfaut.

Detour, *30 mins,*
UZEL-PRÈS-L'OUEST
⌂ ⚒ ▄▄

Go right along the D53 for 2 kilometres. 17th century church; Notre-Dame-de-Bonne-Nouvelle chapel; Saint-Aragon fountain; 17th century houses.

Pass a farm, and follow the farm track opposite. You will rejoin the Hilvern channel, and should make you way up the right bank. When you come to the tarmac road, turn right and then left 150 metres later before joining up again with the right bank of the channel. When you come to the second bridge, cross over to the left bank and then make your way back over to the original side as soon as possible. You will come to a small road, and should veer left through l'Oust and continue along the small road to the Bosméléac dam.

BOSMÉLÉAC DAM
Y

Man-made – 60 hectares in all – the dam was erected in 1832 to feed the Nantes-Brest canal, via which it joins up with the Hilvern channel.

Detour, *45 mins,*
ALLINEUC
⌂ ✕ Y ⚒

Sainte-Anne-de-Langavry chapel and fountain. Kergonan chapel with cross near the church; ruins of Saint-Adrien chapel; Château de la Porte Ohain.

Walk across the dam on the dyke, then turn left and walk round the lake. Take the small road to your left and make your way back down to the edge of the lake as soon as possible. Pass a bridge, and continue on round the reservoir, following the edge of the wood or the meadows as appropriate. Continue along the farm track, and when you get to Kergonan, turn left along a small road. Take the road on the right and continue almost straight on, veering slightly left. At the first crossroads, turn left towards Kerfros and then right towards Les Mares. When you get to the top of the stream, turn left along the gravel path and then turn right to Beau Soleil. Continue straight on into the wood; when you came out the other side, turn left before you enter the meadow. Take the second track on the left, which will bring you out on a tarmac road.

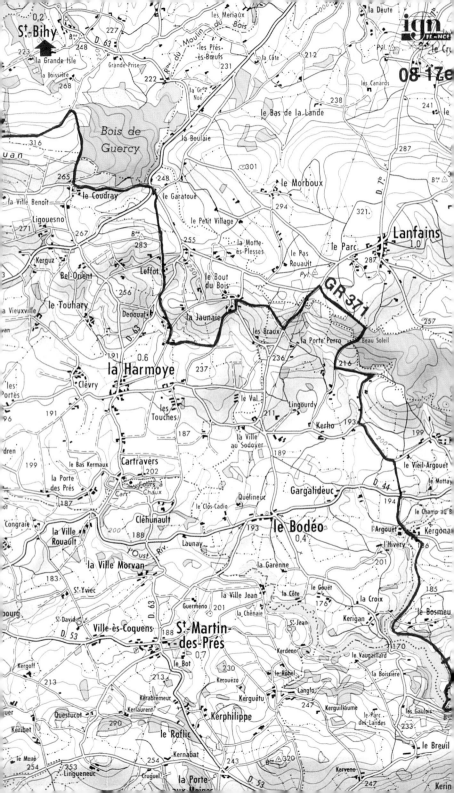

Detour, *15 mins,*
LANFAINS
♟

Take the road on the right.

22.5Km
5:30

Detour, *15 mins,*
LA HARMOYE
⌂ ㅅ ✕ ♨

At Cartravers nearby, there are some old lime kilns.

Detour,
100m to your right
at the crossroads
♟ ♨

LE VIEUX-BOURG
✕ ♟ ♨

The Porzic and Pasquiou standing stones are 3 and 4 kilometres respectively outside the town.

3Km
0.45

Turn left along the tarmac road and make your way up to La Porte Perro, where you turn along the track on your right. When you get to a field, turn left and skirt the large hen houses. Take a left turn again, followed by a right. The first dirt track on the right will take you to a tarmac road.

Follow the small tarmac road on your right, and then veer left towards La Salle. Shortly afterwards, turn right along a dirt track which leads to a meadow; cross the upper half, turn right along the road and then left along the track almost opposite. Go through Leffot and continue straight on. Take the tarmac road on the left for 100 metres until you come to the D790.

Go straight on towards Le Coudray. Turn right when you get to the village and continue straight on to the quarry, which you skirt on the left. Go down the track to the bottom of the quarry, continue opposite and then turn left along the road which runs along the top of the Kerchouan peaks, where the source of the River Gouet is. After the reservoir, turn along the small road on the right and then the track on the left. Turn right past Kerpourcet farm, and then make two left turns. When you come to the village to Troubardou, take the track on the right followed by the one on the left. Cross over a meadow and follow the hedge before continuing along a path that goes over the moor. Climb up to the right until you come to a track, where you should turn left. Turn right at the small road and left along the R16 when you reach the road. This takes you into Le Vieux-Bourg.

Veer right when you enter the town and leave it via the first road on the right. Then turn along the first track on the right. When you come out on a tarmac road, turn right again. Turn left at the big crossroads and right along the dirt track which starts at the house. Turn left along the track and follow the hedge before making your way along the track almost opposite. When the track comes to a dead end, walk through the field following the hedge on the left, until you come to the road. Here you make two right turns and then take the track on the right which leads to Quénéro farm.

Continue past the farm to a lake on your right. Keeping the lake on the left, continue to a tarmac road, where you turn right to the church of Saint-Bihy.

SAINT-BIHY

18th century church; lake.

Continue along the small tarmac road, and then turn left along at track and right at the edge of the field. Continue along the track and turn left to the Gouet. Follow the right-hand bank and the first hedge on the right, which will bring you out at a farm. Follow the track to Bas-Cléden, where you turn left along a small tarmac road which brings you back to the Gouet. Follow the right bank, and then cross over the river 50 metres later on a small wooden bridge. Continue opposite, veering to the right, and climb up to the right until you come to a small stream. Then skirt the field for a few metres before turning along the track on the right and following it to an old farm. Walk past the farm buildings and follow the Gouet downstream. When you come to the second field take the track which climbs gently uphill; when you get to the top turn left. Shortly after you pass a farm, turn right along a small road which narrows to a track. Turn left at the bottom and continue straight on along the wooded path leading to the Château de Robien. (Do not go into the grounds.) Keep on the small tarmac road, then turn left and go straight on to the outskirts of Quintin.

9Km
2:15

QUINTIN

This small city used to be the capital of the weaving industry, and the centre for buying and selling Breton cloth. 17th/18th century Château; La Roche Longue standing stone; Notre-Dame-de-la-Porte fountain; a lake.

Take the Rue du Gasset opposite, the Rue Rochoden and the Rues due Château-Gaillard and Abbé-Fleury. Turn left and right along Rue Notre-Dame. Go down the steps behind the church and continue opposite to the the Gouet. Go past the bridge, turn along the Rue de la Madeleine, and then shortly afterwards turn left down a small tarmac road. When you come to a bend in a road, turn off along the dirt track which runs along the edge of a field and then plunges into the trees. Go to the right, climb up to a track on your left and then follow the dirt track left. This runs along the right bank of the Gouet. A track runs slightly above you, which you should follow to the left. The path will take you across two meadows, and cross the Pas stream over a small bridge. Then take the path opposite. Cross over another meadow and rejoin the Gouet on your left; cross over the small footbridge and

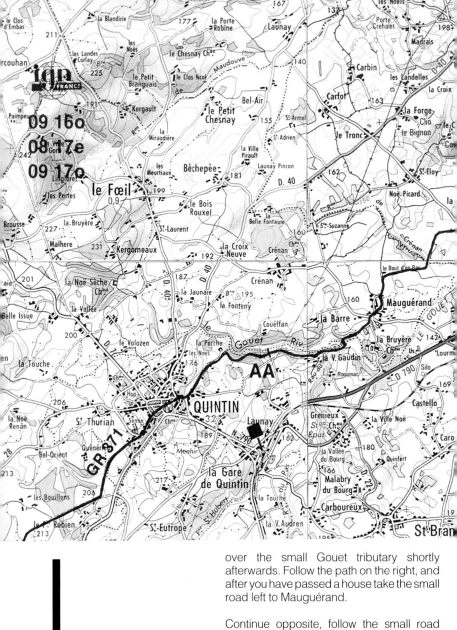

over the small Gouet tributary shortly afterwards. Follow the path on the right, and after you have passed a house take the small road left to Mauguérand.

Continue opposite, follow the small road through the village, and when you come to the T-junction, turn right towards Bout-d'en-Bas. Turn right along the track shortly before you come to the farm, which will later veer left. Carry straight on over wooded slopes following tracks that may at times be rather hidden, and then cross a small stream and a rather muddy patch. Continue opposite diagonally through an abandoned muddy meadow. Then follow the path opposite, which turns into a farm track and comes out on a small road. Turn right and then immediately left at the cross. Cross over the large road and take the first small road on the left. Turn right along a small road and continue along the dirt track. You now have to follow a path, and the start is quite difficult to find. This path veers right, and crosses the Gouet on a stone bridge back to the GR371 shortly afterwards: this was the road you first took out of Saint-Brieuc. Keep the Plaintel and Moncontour fork described earlier on your right. Turn left along a track which narrows to a path. You now retrace part of the route described at the outset in reverse order. Skirt the Gouet through the undergrowth until you come to the Maison des Scouts de France (hut belonging to the French Scouting Association).

6.5Km
1:45

MAISON DES SCOUTS DE FRANCE
⌂

Go to the right of this building on a small path which joins up with the track leading to the house. Cross over this track and go down to the banks of the Gouet, which you should follow downstream along a fisherman's path, keeping as close to it as possible as you cross two meadows. When you come to a footbridge with a ladder at water level, take the small road on the right. Then make two left turns when you come to some houses.

You can see a standing stone in a field, the Château de la Coste in the distance, and a manor house above Sainte-Anne-du-Houlin.

Take the track on your left and then continue opposite, past a farm. Walk along the edge of a wood and then across a meadow to the banks of the Gouet. Follow this again into Sainte-Anne-du-Houlin.

SAINTE-ANNE-DU-HOULIN
Ⓗ ⌂ 𝚼 ⚏

Detour, *30 mins,*
SAINT-JULIEN
✗ ⚏ 🚌 🚃

Go 1.5 kilometres along the D40.

Take the road on the right and then turn immediately left along the track which skirts the Gouet reservoir to Pont-Noir.

6.5Km
1:45

Alternative route to Pont-Noir. Follow the track which runs round the other side of the Gouet reservoir, but which is unmarked. There are more viewing points, but this route is longer.

Pont-Noir

SAINT-BRIEUC YOUTH HOSTEL

⌂

16Km
4:0

Go under the road bridge and continue on round the reservoir. The southern branch of the Saint-Brieuc circular walk described at the beginning of this guide starts 1 kilometre outside Pont-Noir. Cross under the railway viaduct, and keep as close as you can to the reservoir. When you arrive above the dam, go down to the left to the dam, which you can cross over; when you get to the bottom, follow the path which meanders down through the trees. Continue along the small tarmac road, and shortly after the old dam, at the transformer, take the track on the right and cross over a stream. When you come to the T-junction on the plateau, turn left. Go past a pretty little farm with turrets. Turn right immediately after this, and then left on to road. Take the Rue Maurice-Nogues on your right. Turn right 400 metres further on along the Rue Penthièvre until you come to Les Villages church. After the church, cross the car park on the right and continue along a track to the Rue du Vau Gicquel. Turn right and then left after a 100 metres or so into Rue de la Ville-Guyaumard. This takes you on to an old manor house. Very soon after this, you come to the Saint-Brieuc youth hostel.

Opposite the hostel, take a path up to the left around the sports stadium and the municipal gardens. Continue through the woods until you come to a track, and then climb up this to the right. When you come to a fork, follow the gravel track on the right to a group of houses. Follow a fence, turn left when you get to the road, and then left again along Rue Turgot, which is a cul-de-sac. The path on your left will take you through woods, alongside the walls of a private estate. Continue along this path until you come to the Rue de la Fontaine-Brieuc - the actual Brieuc fountain is 20 metres to your right. Turn left and then left again along Rue Vieille-Côte-du-Gouet. Go up steps on the right, cross over the street at the top and climb up the next set of steps. After the Alfred-de-Musset roundabout, take Boulevard Lamartine then the first street on the left, Rue Lesage et Duguesclin, and then successively Rues Christophe-Colomb and Charles-Le-Goffic. You will come out at a dead-end, Rue H.-Pommeret. At the end of this street, take the footpath on your right to a

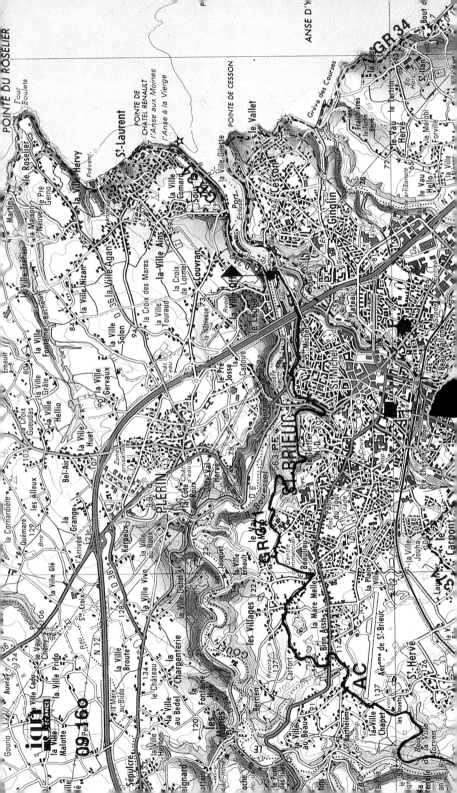

SAINT-BRIEUC

Cathedral; old town

promenade and subsequently to Tertre Aube. At the top of the hill, follow a small path on your left which runs round the houses to another street. Cross the bridge over the dual carriageway and go down a small street to Pont Tournant du Légué. Here you join up with the GR34, which goes towards Erquy and Saint-Malo on the right to Paimpol, Lannion and Morlaix on the left.

INDEX

The many different kinds of accommodation in France are explained in the introduction. Here we include a selection of hotels and other addresses, which is by no means exhaustive — the hotels listed are usually in the one-star of two-star categories. We have given full postal addresses so bookings can be made.

There has been an explosive growth in bed and breakfast facilities (chambres d'hôte) in the past few years, and staying in these private homes can be especially interesting and rewarding. Local shops and the town hall (mairie) can usually direct you to one.

Details of bus/train connections have been provided wherever it was possible. We suggest you refer also to the map inside the front cover.